Racquetball:
A Primer

Cheryl Norton, Ed.D.
Assistant Professor of Physical Education
Metropolitan State College, Denver

James E. Bryant, Ed.D.
Professor of Physical Education
Metropolitan State College, Denver

Morton Publishing Company
925 W. Kenyon Ave., Unit 4
Englewood, Colorado 80110

Acknowledgments

The contributions of several individuals and groups provided the necessary input for completion of this text.

Jane Kober, assistant professor, Metropolitan State College, is acknowledged for her insight and creative thought associated with the chapter on drills for the aspiring player. Ron McCall, Joni McCall and Tom Furjanic contributed the time, skills, and efforts as models for the numerous photographs of skill sequences and play situations. The illustrations, prepared by Darryl Wisnia, added greatly to the understanding of the material concerning various strategies, court dimensions, and drills.

The Aurora Athletic Club is recognized for permitting photographs to be taken of skill and play situations in its club. Hagan Sports Ltd. is acknowledged for permitting photographs to be shot of its racquetball equipment displays.

Preface

Racquetball: A Primer is designed for the novice and beginning player attempting to develop skills in racquetball. The text is divided into ten chapters that deal with the basics of racquetball.

The first two chapters present information on equipment, safety, preliminaries to the strokes in racquetball and an introduction to the game of racquetball. Chapters three and four introduce the various offensive and defensive strokes used in playing racquetball. These are the basic strokes that enable the player to engage in a competitive experience. Chapter five provides information on putting the ball in play by serving the ball, and chapter six introduces how to cope with the back wall and the corners of the racquetball court when the ball is in play. Chapters seven and eight serve as a culmination of the first six chapters by providing insight on how to put all the strokes together in a plan of offensive and defensive strategy.

Chapter nine and ten complete the overall view of a primer for racquetball. Chapter nine gives insight on drills that provides the student with drills for practice. Chapter ten establishes the basis to the game by introducing the rules and etiquette of racquetball.

The text is an appropriate introduction to racquetball for the novice player and it will serve as a guide to enable the novice to develop both physical and mental skills needed to succeed in racquetball. Through the use of photographs and illustrations the concept of the game is visually presented to aid in comprehending the skills of the game. The summary sections entitled "points to remember" and "common errors and why you make them" enhance the learning experience for the player. Overall, the text provides a solid primer of information and insight for the novice or beginning player.

Table of Contents

Chapter One

Court, Equipment, and Safety

Racquetball is played in an enclosed court using the four walls, floor, and ceiling as the playing surface. In areas where a four-wall court cannot be built, one- or three-wall racquetball may be played. The rules and strategy for all these games are similar. This text, however, will concentrate only on the more complex, four-wall game.

The dimensions and markings on the court are as shown below. Fortunately, the terminology used to describe the court is easily learned: floor, ceiling, front, back, and side walls. The floor lines identify the *service zone* boundaries. The only other mark on the court denotes the *receiving line* for the player returning the serve.

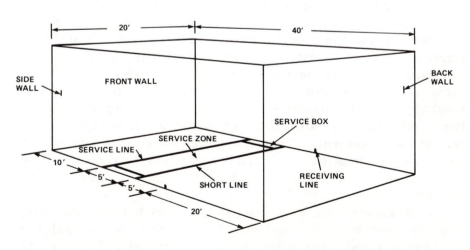

Dimensions and markings on a racquetball court.

The court can also be divided into four main areas of play.

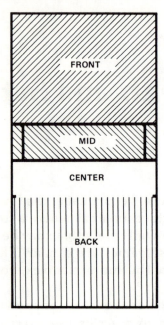

Designated floor areas on the court.

Brief Overview of the Game

The object of the game of racquetball is to score 21 points before your opponent does. Only the serving player scores points. A point is scored when the server's opponent fails to hit the ball to the front wall before the ball touches the floor twice. If the server fails to return the ball to the front wall, he/she loses serve. In this way, service (and the opportunity to score) is alternated until one player or team accumulates 21 points and wins the game.

Racquetball may be played with two (singles), three (cut-throat), or four (doubles) players. In singles, one player opposes another player, and in doubles, one two-person team plays another two-person team. However, in cut-throat, a single server plays against two opponents. When the server loses serve, one of the opponents becomes the server and plays against the remaining two players. The first player to earn 21 points during his/her serve is the winner.

In all games, each rally (exchange of hits between opposing players) is begun with a *legal serve*. For the serve to be legal, the server must stand in the service zone, drop the ball to the floor, and strike it on the rebound so that it hits the front wall before any other court surface. The front wall rebound may not touch the floor in front of or on the short line. Before the ball hits the floor, it may rebound off one side wall but not off the ceiling, back wall, or both side walls. However, the return of serve and any other hit may rebound the ball off any surface except the floor before reaching the front wall. Service is changed when the server fails to keep the ball in play or he/she does not serve legally. If the receiver fails to return the ball to the front wall, a point is scored.

Outfitting for Play

Dress: The usual dress for both men and women includes a sports shirt or T-shirt and shorts. All clothes must be white or light colored. The rules of play forbid dark colors, since they may interfere with the sighting of the ball.

Head or wristbands aid in the absorption of perspiration around the head and hands and are optional to wear. Shirts will help to absorb body perspiration and must be worn at all times during play. Body perspiration dripping onto the floor of the court provides a potential hazard to fast-moving feet.

Shoes: The footwear worn on a racquetball court should be an athletic shoe (like a tennis shoe) that supports shifting body weight

Proper dress for racquetball.

Racquetball head and wrist bands.

and lateral movement on the court. Shoes designed for jogging/running should never be used. Dark-soled shoes are forbidden as well because the sole mars the court surface. Finally, adequate socks or foot cover will prevent the foot from sliding in the shoe and irritating the skin.

Gloves: The use of a glove is optional and dependent upon your comfort and need. Many players wear a glove on their racquet hand to help maintain a better grip on the racquet and prevent the racquet from slipping from their hand.

Athletic shoe suitable for racquetball.

Racquetball gloves.

Goggles: Although protective eyewear is not regulated through the official rules of racquetball, many courts maintain a policy of having to wear goggles to play. Severe eye damage, including detached retinas and the loss of vision, have followed direct eye hits with either the ball or the racquet. Goggles can be bought to wear over eyeglasses or to protect the eye itself. Goggles are a *necessity* to insure safe play.

Ball: Specifications for a racquetball ball are determined by the American Amateur Racquetball Association. Balls come in either black, red, green, or blue. Choose the color that your eyes follow best.

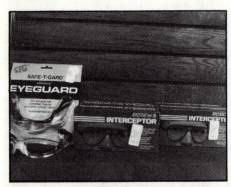
Protective goggles.

Racquetball balls.

Recently, pressurized balls that can be inflated to a specified pressure have been used in games. Consequently, they are often overinflated and are very "lively" during play. Beginning players should not learn the game of racquetball with this type of ball.

Racquets: The selection of a racquet is dependent upon your style of play and the amount of money you want to invest. The frame of a racquet is either constructed of a metal such as aluminum or steel or is a composite of high-technology fibers such as graphite, boron, and fiberglass. The metal racquets cost less to make and are usually more durable but do not have the flexibility of the composite racquet. Because of their stiffness, aluminum racquets are more popular for players who choose a power game over a controlled "placement" game. The composite racquets, on the other hand, are flexible and keep the ball on the strings longer, thus providing more control over the ball placement.

Both types of racquets are very light in weight, usually tipping the scale at between 8 and 10 ounces. The less arm strength you have, the lighter the racquet you should use.

Selection of racquets.

Grip Size: As a rule of thumb, the grip size should be smaller than that of a tennis racquet. Most experts suggest that when gripping the racquet properly, the middle finger of the racquet hand should just touch the palm to allow for a good wrist snap.

Racquet Strings and Tension: Racquets are usually already strung when you buy them. The two types of materials commonly used to make strings are nylon and gut. Gut has very little advantage over a good nylon string. If anything, gut tends to wear out faster and must be replaced more often.

If you must have your racquet restrung, you can specify the amount of tension on the strings. Tension levels vary from 23 pounds (fiberglass racquets) to 33 or 35 pounds (metal racquets). On the average, most players opt for a tension level between 26 and 28 pounds. The more tension on the racquet strings, the faster the ball will rebound off the racquet; consequently, the more control the player must have to accurately place the ball. Therefore, beginning players who have trouble controlling shots should string their racquets with less tension.

Handle and Thong: Racquet handles are made of rubber or leather. Although leather is more expensive, it usually allows you to grip the racquet more securely.

To be legal, each racquet must have a *thong* attached to the handle. The thong is a safety cord that is worn on the wrist during play. Replacement thongs may be purchased where racquetball equipment is supplied.

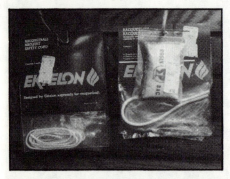
Replacement safety thongs.

Care: Racquets are easy to care for if you use some common sense. Try not to leave your racquet in the backseat of your car. Extremes in heat or cold will cause the strings to become brittle or break down faster. Keep a cover on the racquet to prevent objects from catching in the strings. If your strings are breaking frequently, you can have plastic eyelets inserted where the string wraps around the frame to protect the strings from wearing on the edge.

Safety on the Court

Safety on the court begins when you walk onto the court, put on your goggles, and shut the door to protect against people walking in during play. During play, a racquetball court is safe only if all the players are courteous. This means staying out of your opponent's path to the ball or arm swing. Similary, no shot is "too good to pass up" if a player is in the path of your swing. There is no excuse for hitting another player with your racquet. If he/she were that close to you, your shot could not have been clear. In addition, learn to play the strokes correctly. Too many players keep their tennis stroke alive in the racquetball court. Wide swings from the shoulder require the room that a tennis court provides. There is no place on the racquetball court for this kind of play.

Hitting a ball when your opponent is in the way.

Each racquet must have a thong or safety cord attached to it. This cord is worn around the wrist of the playing hand to prevent the racquet from flying out of the hand of the player and injuring someone on the court. This cord must be used at all times.

Finally, you should continually be aware of player's movement on the court. Stay out of the way of the player hitting the ball, and when it is your turn to hit, take your shot only if it is clear. Most balls are hit from the back of the court forward. If you are in front of the ball, DO NOT turn completely around to "see" what is going on behind you in the back court. This not only exposes your chest and abdomen to a hard-hit ball, but it leaves your face unprotected. Rather, you should angle your body slightly so that you can see the back court with your peripheral vision and hold the racquet to protect your face as you look through the strings. Using the racquet to protect your face from an oncoming ball is an effective safety measure only if the racquet "beats" the ball to the target. Don't rely on your reflexes to "get the racquet" up in time to protect your face. As a precaution, always use your racquet as a shield if your face is exposed to the ball's path, and wear your goggles to protect your eyes against the stray shot. This way you can play the game and finish "looking" the same way as when you entered the court.

Protecting your face by looking through the racquet strings.

Player not leaving center court to give opponent clear shot off a back wall rebound.

You should be aware that experienced players will let the ball rebound off the back wall before playing it. This means that a center court position needs to be held open for him/her to follow the ball. Anticipate the most direct path to the ball that your opponent can take, and keep that court position clear. Racquetball is not a game that allows mental lapses. Each player must know where the ball is at all times and where other players are moving.

Should you interfere with your opponent's movement on the court, completion of his/her swing, or get hit with his/her racquet, a *hinder* must be called. A hinder should be called by the offended party in a recreational game and by a referee during tournament play. When a hinder is called, play is stopped and the point re-played from the serve. Contact does not have to occur for a hinder to occur. Preferably, play should stop before players or racquets collide to avoid potential injury.

Safety is a matter of habit and thinking: protect yourself by wearing goggles, using your racquet as a shield, keeping your thong on your wrist, and closing the door of the court when playing. Anticipate your opponent's position, the path of the ball, and the movement of players on the court. Most important, remember that racquetball is just a game, and one point is not worth risking your health or that of your opponent just to "make a shot."

Chapter Two

Introduction and Preliminaries to the Strokes in Racquetball

Being properly prepared to hit the ball is essential to the correct execution of offensive and defensive shots. This includes warming up, properly gripping the racquet, assuming the set or ready position, and pivoting to either a forehand or backhand hitting position.

Getting Ready to Participate: the Warm-Up

A good rule of thumb to follow for any exercise in which you engage is "never take your body by surprise." A warm-up to prepare yourself mentally and physically allows your body to smoothly "shift gears" from inactivity to activity. The stress of sudden activity causes your body to rely on reserve energy sources rather than energy derived from breathing oxygen. Using up your reserve energy at the start of the exercise means that you will fatigue more quickly, and you will have to quit the activity or your level of play will decline.

The warm-up should consist of three phases: relaxation, stretching, and increased heart activity. Relaxation is needed to relieve internal stress. The body responds to stress by increasing muscle tension. Tight muscles work in opposition to the free and fluid movement needed for any exercise/sport activity. In addition, stretching exercises will be more effective if the muscles are relaxed.

Stretching is the second phase of the warm-up. It is important to help increase your ease and range of movement. Since racquetball is literally a game of inches, the ability to extend your reach to its limit may "make up" for slowly reacting to the ball's action.

Getting ready to play: relaxing, stretching, increasing your heart rate.

Another important function of this phase is to help alleviate residual soreness from previous racquetball sessions and avoid further injury to tight muscles that may have resulted from the sudden movements required by the game.

The last phase of the warm-up should increase your heart rate. This activity will also increase the body's available energy. As a result, at the beginning of the game, the reserve energy stores are not depleted. Playing racquetball will "feel" more comfortable, and you will not tire as rapidly.

These three warm-up activities are done in sequence immediately before entering the court to play. Many people make the mistake of warming up and then waiting for 5 to 10 minutes before playing racquetball. Consequently, most of the effect of the warm-up is lost. The increase in heart rate will decline within one to two minutes after the warm-up is over. Therefore, no time should be wasted getting onto the court.

Last but not least is mental preparation for play. Unless your mind is relaxed and focused on the sport ahead, your body cannot respond properly to the challenge of the game. Concentrate on the game to be played rather than other current "events" in your life so your skills can be used to their fullest.

Holding the Racquet: the Grips

The power in a racquetball stroke comes from the snap of the wrist that occurs when the ball is contacted. Unless the racquet is gripped in such a way as to maximize this snap, the potential power of a stroke will be lost. There are two basic grips that most players adapt to their style of play and a third that some use in special situations. The first, and easily the most popular, is the Eastern Forehand. The Eastern Forehand, as its name implies, is used to hit only shots on the racquet-hand (forehand) side of the body. Its counterpart on the non-racquet-hand side is the Eastern Backhand and will be discussed later.

The easiest way to assume an Eastern Forehand grip is merely to hold the racquet on edge so that it is perpendicular to the floor and then "shake hands" with the handle. In the shaking hands

Shaking hands with the racquet.

position, the first finger and thumb of the racquet hand should form a "V" along the top of the racquet, the point of the "V" lying on the midline of the handle's surface. The fingers are spread in a "trigger or pistol grip" position to allow for better wrist snap.

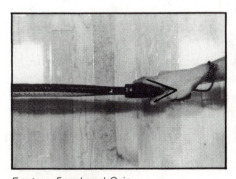

Eastern Forehand Grip.

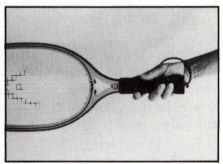

Trigger or Finger Grip.

Another way to assume this position is to hold the racquet in the non-racquet hand so that the racquet is again on edge. Place your racquet hand with fingers spread on the strings of the racquet so that the palm is flat against the racquet face. Slide your racquet

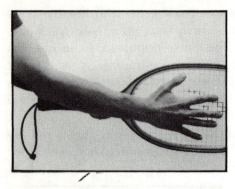

Palm flat on racquet face.

hand down the racquet until the end of the handle meets the end of your palm, and wrap your fingers around the handle. Again you should check to see if the "V" formed by your first finger and thumb is pointed properly along the top surface of the handle. Be careful not to grip the racquet so that the handle lies perpendicular to your fingers in a "fist" grip or the wrist snap will be lost. If you

Assuming the Eastern Forehand grip.

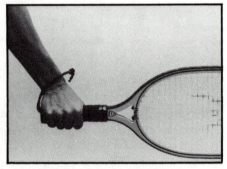

Improper grip on racquet, fingers perpendicular to handle.

turn the racquet over so that your palm is pointed toward the ceiling of the court and open your hand, a racquet in the correct position should lie diagonally across the palm. The handle should cover the first knuckle of the first finger and the bottom left side of the palm.

Handle of racquet lies diagonally across palm of hand.

If you use this grip for your forehand shots, you must change your grip to hit backhand shots (shots to the non-racquet-hand side). This is due to the way in which the arm moves about the elbow. The construction of the elbow joint causes the forearm to move only up and down (flex and extend) when the arm is held straight at your side. When hitting a backhand shot, the racquet arm is pulled across the body and then extended. If the hand is held in its normal position in line with the elbow, the racquet head will be turned up and will hit the ball at an angle with the extension. Thus, shots that should be hit straight into the wall will be "popped," or hit up toward the ceiling. To hit a level backhand shot, you must change your grip from the Eastern Forehand to the Eastern Backhand grip. To find this position on your racquet, assume the forehand grip just discussed and hold the racquet on edge. With your non-racquet hand, turn the top of the racquet toward the palm of your hand so that the forefinger-thumb "V" falls below the top left edge of the racquet. This grip rotates the

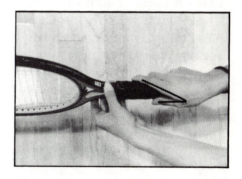

Eastern Backhand Grip.

head of the racquet downward to compensate for the elbow's inability to rotate and allows you to hit a level ball. The problem with changing from the forehand to the backhand grip is that it takes TIME. Thus, it is important that you immediately recognize when a backhand shot should be hit to give you as much time as possible to make the switch. A similar problem occurs after the backhand shot is taken. The grip must be changed back to the forehand placement. Unfortunately, many players have difficulty changing grips and hitting the ball too! But a player must do something to change the angle of the racquet head!

One alternative solution to this problem is to simply rotate the wrist forward when hitting a backhand shot. This turns the racquet head downward and allows a flat shot to be hit. Returning to the Eastern Forehand grip only takes a "twist" of the wrist. The major

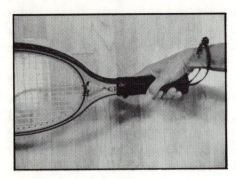

Rotating wrist forward to turn racquet face down.

problem with this method is that it is so easy, new players often FORGET to do it!

Either way of changing the racquet position for a backhand can be effective as long as you consistently use it. Choose one method and practice with it all the time.

A second alternative to changing grips is to avoid using the Eastern Forehand and Backhand grips completely. Instead, use the Continental grip. In the Continental grip, the racquet is held in a position midway between the Eastern Forehand and Backhand. To assume this grip, the racquet must be rotated one-eighth of a turn from the Eastern Forehand toward the forehand side. Now the "V" will point to the top left edge of the handle. Thus, with the

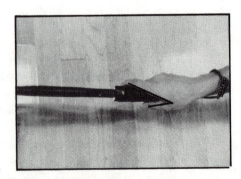

Continental Grip.

Continental grip, little or no adjustment must be made for either a forehand or backhand shot, although the wrist may be slightly rotated clockwise to adjust the face of the racquet to hit a level ball.

The third grip is called the Western grip or "frying pan" grip. It is similar to the grip you use on a frying pan handle when you lift the pan off a stove or pick your racquet up off the floor. This grip is

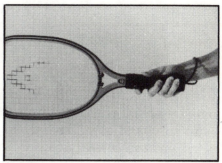

Western Grip.

used ONLY for overhead forehand shots. However, new players often use this grip on all shots and consequently have difficulty hitting low shots.

After hitting a few balls, always recheck your grip to make sure that the racquet has not twisted in your hand. Some players will even mark the "V" placement of the thumb and forefinger on the racquet's top edge with tape. This helps to guide the correct hand positioning.

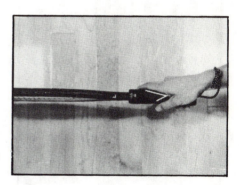

*Eastern Forehand Grip marked
with a "V" on the racquet.*

Points to Remember:

1. Note the position of the "V" on the racquet handle and make sure that it matches your hand placement.
2. Keep your fingers spread out in a pistol or trigger finger grip — do not keep a fist grip on the handle.
3. Change to a backhand grip or compensate for the elbow's movement by rotating the wrist to hit a ball on the non-racquet side. Change back to a forehand grip after the shot has been taken.
4. Overhead shots may be hit using a Western grip.
5. Continental grip may be used to hit all balls.

Set, Pivot, and Stroke

The Set

The set or "ready" position prepares you to hit the ball. Begin each stroke at the set position and return to it following each hit. The set position allows you to move quickly to hit a ball with either your forehand or backhand.

To get in the set position, stand with your feet shoulder width apart, toes pointing forward and weight equally balanced on the balls of the feet. The racquet should be held in front of you at waist height, and a forehand grip should be used. Your non-racquet hand should help to support the racquet. Knees should be slightly bent and pointed forward. Shoulders, head, and neck are relaxed, with your eyes free to follow the movement of the ball. Breathing must be deep and regular.

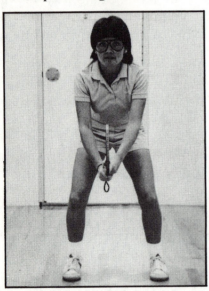
Set Position — front view.

Set Position — side view.

Points to Remember:

1. Face the front wall, with toes pointed forward.
2. Weight is equally balanced on the balls of the feet, which are placed shoulder width apart.
3. Hold the racquet with a forehand grip at waist height in front of you.
4. Knees are bent, and the body is ready to "spring" into action.

The Pivot

As soon as you have decided if the ball is to be hit with a forehand or backhand stroke, you must PIVOT or turn your body to prepare for the hit. The sooner the decision can be made, the better prepared you will be to hit the ball. So decide QUICKLY. The importance of the pivot is that it turns the hips sideways to the front wall. This allows for the player to "step into" the ball and add his/her body weight into the power of the stroke. A baseball batter

Pivot position for forehand stroke.   Stepping into the ball from a
pivot position.

will take the same position. Except to bunt, the batter will always stand sideways to the pitcher and step into the pitch by shifting his weight forward. Thus, the ball can be hit with more force. Similarly, the pivot in racquetball positions you to step into the ball, shift your weight, and increase the power of your stroke. This is especially important for women players who may have weak arms and wrists.

The pivot itself may be done in either of two ways. In both methods, you must put your weight on one foot and turn on that foot to face a side wall. Your free foot will either be pulled forward or behind you to complete the pivot. In either case, your body should finish with your hips facing a side wall. Whether you pivot and step forward or backward depends on where the ball rebounds and whether you have to move up or back to reach it. Further adjustments in body position can be made by "cross-stepping" forward or backward. During any pivot motion, your eyes must not lose contact with the ball, and your face should be directed toward the ball.

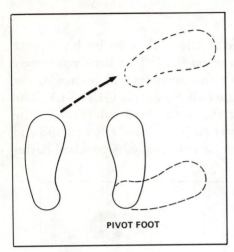

Forward Pivot.

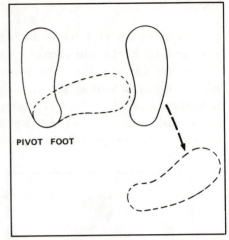

Backstep Pivot.

Points to Remember:

1. Decide quickly where the ball is to be hit, and pivot to that side immediately.
2. After the pivot, the body should face a sidewall.
3. Move either forward or backward to the ball by cross-stepping up or back.
4. Keep your eyes and face directed at the ball.

Forehand Stroke

The only problem remaining is to hit the ball! Forehand strokes will be discussed first, then additional information on backhand strokes will be given. The forehand stroke itself begins as the racquet is carried from the set stance through the position change that results from the pivot.

BACKSWING

As the body is turned to the side wall, so is the racquet. But the racquet continues to be pulled back so that with the elbow bent, the racquet is in a line between your body and the back wall. This is called the backswing. In this position, the racquet is held almost at right angles to the forearm, which serves to "cock" the wrist.

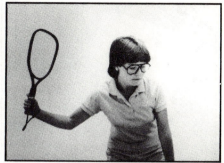

Completed backswing with racquet in line between the back wall and your body.   *Wrist cock on the backswing.*

WRIST COCK

The wrist cock is a critical part of your stroke. It is the "uncocking" or snapping of the wrist and racquet at the ball which generates the speed and power of the stroke. Without cocking the wrist, as in pulling the hammer back in a gun, there would be no way of hitting the ball with an explosive force. To be most effective, the snap or "uncocking" of the wrist must occur when the ball is contacted.

FORWARD SWING

As you prepare to swing the racquet forward, you must first shift your weight forward. This is done by stepping into the path of the ball with the foot closest to the front wall. At the same time, the forward swing of the racquet is begun by extending the elbow (i.e., straightening out the arm). It is important that during the swing, the elbow remain close to the side of the body. This position enables the ball to be contacted below waist level and prevents "over-the-shoulder" shots. Once the arm is extended, the racquet should be at the same level off the floor as your hand, with the head perpendicular to the floor, or "on edge." However, the racquet hand should lead the racquet through the swing. This position helps to maintain a "cocked" wrist through the swing.

Forward swing maintaining wrist cock.

Points to Remember:

1. On the backswing, pull the racquet back to a point directly behind you in line with your body and the back wall.
2. Hold the racquet almost at right angles to the forearm to "cock" the wrist.
3. Shift weight to your forward foot.
4. Extend the arm on the forward swing, holding the upper arm close to the body.
5. Maintain wrist cock through the swing, with the racquet head trailing the wrist and hand through the swing.
6. Keep the racquet head perpendicular to the floor and at the same level as the hand.

CONTACT

Contact with the ball should be made slightly in front of the forward foot as your weight is shifted forward. At the point of impact, the wrist is snapped. Contact with the ball should be made as close to the ground as possible, with your arm extended. To do this, you must bend your knees to drop your waist and racquet close to the ground.

Weight shifted forward and swinging to hit ball off of forward foot.

The ball can be contacted at one of three points during its flight: (1) as it rebounds off the front wall, dropping below your waist toward the floor; (2) after the ball rebounds off the floor and bounces toward your racquet; and (3) after the ball reaches the height of its bounce and is falling back to the floor and below your waist. For experienced players, hitting the ball as it rebounds off the

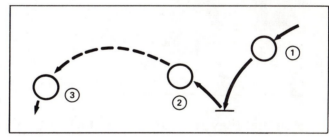

Points of contact for a rebounding ball.

floor maintains a fast tempo in the game. The beginning player, however, should wait for the ball to reach the height of its bounce and begin to rebound to the floor for the second time before hitting the ball.

Points to Remember:

1. Shift your weight onto your forward foot at the beginning of the forward swing.
2. Hit the ball slightly in front of your forward foot when it is below waist level.
3. At the point of impact, snap the wrist.
4. If possible, contact the ball low to the ground, just before it would hit the floor for the second time.

FOLLOW-THROUGH

A mistake that many beginners make is failing to complete the stroke, or to "follow through" after the hit is made. Consequently, these players "punch" at the ball with a shortened stroke and lose the force of their hit. The follow-through made after contact with the ball allows for the completion of the stroke and hitting the ball with all the force of your swing. It also allows you to recover from the stroke quickly and adjust your stance back to the set position to await your next hit.

In general, a racquetball stroke should end with the racquet swung past the midline of the body and finish in front of the forward leg. The follow-through should rotate the shoulders and

Follow-through of the forehand stroke.

hips so that they are again facing the front wall, with the front foot acting as a pivot. At the end of the stroke, your weight should be concentrated on your forward foot but balanced so that you do not fall down. During this follow-through, the body should be kept low to the ground. Standing up too quickly will cause the ball to be "carried" upward with your movement and make it difficult for you to hit low balls.

Points to Remember:

1. Follow the stroke through to the end of the swing.
2. Stay low; keep the racquet low.
3. After the ball has been contacted, allow the body to rotate toward the front wall following the direction of the arm swing.
4. Don't stand up until the follow-through is complete.

Backhand Stroke

To hit a backhand stroke, use either a backhand grip on the racquet, or turn the racquet face down by rotating the wrist. The movement begins as the forehand stroke from the set position. The pivot, however, results in the player facing the opposite side wall. Again, the pivot can be made by either stepping forward or backward, depending on the position of the ball (see page 20). After pivoting, the hips should be parallel to the side wall.

Set position before backhand.

Backhand pivot with the hips facing the side wall.

BACKSWING

The backhand stroke is begun by pulling the racquet across the body with the backswing. At the end of the backswing, the racquet is held in line between your shoulder and the back wall. In this position, the upper body must rotate more than in the forehand

Backswing position for backhand stroke.

stroke in order for the racquet to be positioned behind the shoulder. When correctly rotated, the chin should almost rest on the shoulder of the racquet arm.

WRIST COCK

The racquet must be held with the wrist cocked, as in the forehand stroke. In the cocked position, the racquet is almost at a 90-degree angle to the forearm.

Wrist cock.

FORWARD SWING

As the forward swing is begun, the player's weight is shifted to the front foot. The racquet face should be held at the same level as

Forward swing with the racquet trailing the hand.

the hand, with the racquet head trailing the hand on the forward swing to maintain the cocked position. The elbow should be held close to the body. In error, a beginning player often extends the elbow out away from the body. Consequently, power is lost, and often the ball is rebounded to the side of the court instead of forward as the racquet is pulled diagonally across the body.

Points to Remember:

1. Use a backhand grip, or rotate your wrist to change the position of the racquet head to hit the ball.
2. Pivot to the opposite side wall from that turned to with the forehand stroke.
3. Pull the racquet back to a position between the shoulder and the back wall.
4. Cock the wrist at the end of the backswing.
5. On the forward swing, keep your upper arm and elbow close to the body.
6. Keep the racquet head behind the hand on the forward swing.

CONTACT

To contact the ball, your weight should be forward on the front foot. Extend the elbow at the point of contact so that the racquet

Contacting the ball.

almost pivots around the extended arm. The racquet should contact the ball just in front of the forward foot as low to the ground as possible. When the ball is contacted, the wrist is snapped sharply to increase the impact on the ball.

Points to Remember:

1.   Your weight is shifted forward at contact with the ball.
2.   Hit the ball when it is just in front of your forward foot and close to the ground.
3.   At the point of contact, extend the arm, keeping the elbow close to the body.
4.   As the racquet hits the ball, snap the wrist to increase the power in your stroke.

FOLLOW-THROUGH

As with the forehand, the backhand stroke is finished with a follow-through. With the follow-through, the chest and hips end up facing the front wall, and the racquet is swung to a point opposite the shoulder of the racquet arm. Without a follow-through, the strength of the swing is lost. Until the stroke is complete, keep your head down to prevent yourself from standing up before the ball

Follow-through.

leaves the racquet. Otherwise the ball will be lifted up with your movement.

Points to Remember:

1. Finish the stroke with a follow-through so that the racquet stops at a point opposite the forward shoulder.
2. Stay low after hitting the ball.

The success of either a forehand or backhand stroke is dependent upon your ability to hit the ball consistently with the same stroking motion. This means that the point of contact with the ball in relation to your body must not vary. The ony way to assure this is to MOVE on the court so that the ball is aligned properly with your stroke. Too many beginning players (and some better ones, too!) are content to hit the ball regardless of where it is, if it is within their reach. This tactic results in many unorthodox strokes in an attempt to hit the ball. Since most of these shots have never been practiced, these strokes merely rebound the ball back to the front wall rather than being accurately placed. It is the player who positions him/herself consistently to hit the same shot who can make conscious changes in the racquet head angle or force of impact to DIRECT the ball away from the opponent's reach. Now THAT is racquetball!

Common Errors and Why You Make Them

1. I never know where the ball is going.
    A. You fail to position yourself so that the ball is contacted at the same place in relation to your body at all times. Move in the court, and go to where the ball will be. Set yourself up, and hit the ball as you have practiced.
2. I can't hit the ball hard.
    A. Check to see if you are following through rather than just "punching" at the ball and stopping your arm motion.
    B. Make sure that you are snapping your wrist at the moment of contact with the ball to increase the impact.

(Continued on page 30)

Common Errors and Why You Make Them (Cont.)

    C.   Check to make sure that you are hitting the ball when it is still in front of you, i.e., off your front foot rather than behind your front foot.

3.   The ball always goes "up." I can't seem to hit a low ball.

    A.   Check your grip to see if the racquet head is pointed up at contact.

    B.   Watch your body position to see if you are standing up before the ball leaves the racquet head. You may be "carrying" the ball up with you.

    C.   Emphasize a follow-through rather than just punching at the ball.

4.   I miss the ball completely, or the ball always hits a side wall.

    A.   You are probably hitting the ball behind your front foot. This area is not in your field of vision, and you lose track of the ball. Hitting the ball from this position also means that your arm has not swung the racquet so that the racquet head is parallel to the front wall. Instead, the racquet head is still angled toward a side wall, causing the ball to rebound in that direction.

5.   I hit the ball into the side wall.

    A.   Usually this means that you have not changed from the set position to the pivot. Your hips are therefore facing the front wall rather than the side wall. As a result, your stroke comes across the body and directs the ball into the side wall.

6.   I can't hit my backhand with strength and power.

    A.   You are positioning yourself too close to the balls on your backhand side. You have to keep the racquet close to your body and cannot extend your arm as you swing to contact the ball with power. Also, you could be holding your elbow away from your body as you make your forward swing. This would also prevent you from extending your arm to hit the ball.

Chapter 3

Offensive Strokes

An offensive shot is designed to win a point outright by virtue of the skill with which it is hit. Regardless of where your opponent is playing, the well-executed offensive shot should always be a winner. Several basic offensive shots exist. Any offensive shot may be hit with either a forehand or backhand stroke, and the skilled player can use either stroke with equal effectiveness.

The beginning player will usually choose to hit an offensive shot from his/her forehand side. This gives credence to the observation of a player having a "weak" side, i.e., one from which an offensive shot is usually not hit (in most cases the backhand). Therefore, a good strategy to follow when playing a *"weak"-sided* opponent is to hit your offensive shots so that they must be returned with a "weak" side shot (i.e., backhand). With this strategy, if your offensive shot is not "perfect," you are usually not setting up an offensive return.

The type of offensive shot you hit is dependent upon your skill with each shot, your position on the court, and in a few instances, your opponent's court position. To hit accurate offensive shots requires hours of practice on the court. Therefore, you should not rely on offensive shots in a game situation until you can hit them consistently in practice.

Kill Shots

A kill shot is the ultimate offensive weapon of a racquetball player. By definition, a kill shot is a ball that hits the front wall so low and hard that the rebound to the floor occurs almost simultaneously with the front-wall hit. This rebound makes it virtually impossible for your opponent to return the ball even if he/she is standing in the ball's path.

Rebound of a kill shot off the front wall.

All kill shots, except the overhead kill, should be hit when the ball is close to the floor. Contact with the ball must be made by bending your knees to drop your waist and racquet arm close to the floor. Ideally, the ball should be struck when it is positioned between your bent knee and the top of your foot. The shot is then made with

Racquet position off the court to hit a kill shot.

a normal forehand or backhand motion, with emphasis on generating power in the hit by stepping into the ball and using a good wrist snap. The harder the ball is hit, the farther away from the front

Forehand kill shot sequence.

Backhand kill shot sequence.

wall a kill shot can be successfully made. Most beginners, however, because of their weaker stroke, should concentrate on hitting kill shots from a mid court position or just behind the short line.

The critical factor in hitting a good kill shot is keeping the racquet perpendicular to the floor and the swing parallel to the floor to insure hitting a flat or level ball. A level hit will rebound off the

Racquet head perpendicular to the floor on a kill shot.

Sequence of kill shot showing racquet head perpendicular to floor.

front wall at or below the height that it hits into the wall. Thus, a low, level ball hit to the front wall has the greatest potential for achieving the desired kill shot effect.

Front Wall-Straight-In Kill Shot

A front wall-straight-in kill shot hits the front wall first and rebounds toward the back wall without touching a side wall. This shot can be hit from anyplace in the court and at anytime during play, but it is most effective if your opponent is next to (A) or behind you (B) in the court. Ideally, this kill shot should be directed toward the half of the front wall farthest away from the opposing player. Since the ball follows a straight path to the front wall, the racquet face must be parallel to this surface when it strikes the ball. In addition, keeping the swing level to the floor will insure that the ball is hit low to the front wall.

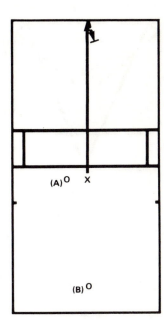

*Front wall straight-in
kill shot.*

Front Wall-Side Wall Kill (Corner)

If the opponent is in the back court or close to a side wall, a front wall-side wall kill may be used. In this shot, the racquet is held so that the face is aimed at a corner of the front wall. As a result, the ball will hit the front wall close to the front wall-side wall crotch and quickly rebound to the nearest side wall. Depending upon the angle with which the ball is hit, the ball may bounce toward a front- or mid-court position. The success of this shot depends on

*Racquethead angled to front corner
for kill shot.*

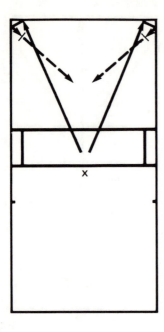

*Front wall - Side wall kill
(corner).*

your opponent's court position and how accurately you can hit the ball. If the ball is not hit low as a kill shot should be, or if the opponent is not far enough in the back court or toward a side wall, the shot will be a setup for an easy return to the front wall. One way to adjust for a quick-reacting opponent who covers the court well is to hit the corner kill at a sharper angle so that the ball rebounds toward the front-court position.

Side Wall-Front Wall (Pinch Kill)

The pinch kill shot hits one side wall before rebounding into the front wall. An advantage of hitting the pinch kill rather than the corner kill is simply the placement of the rebounding ball. Where the corner kill is more likely to rebound close to a mid-court position, the pinch kill rebounds tightly into a front corner. However, to be most effective with the pinch kill, the opponent should be next to or behind you in the court. Whether the shot is directed to the left or right front corner depends partly on your position in the court, but more importantly on your opponent's position. Ideally, you should always hit the ball so that the rebound off the front wall is traveling away from the opponent. If this can't be done, then at least hit the ball so that it rebounds toward the opponent's

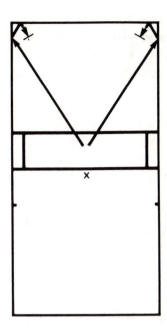

*Side wall - Front wall
kill (pinch).*

weak side. A shot to the weak side, even if not perfectly hit, should not result in an offensive return.

To hit a pinch kill (as with the corner kill), the racquet face upon contact with the ball must be angled to the side wall rather than

Pinch kill away from opponent.

held parallel to the front wall. The ball must be contacted close to the ground. To do this, bend your knees, drop your waist, and extend your racquet arm down. In all other respects, the technique for hitting this kill shot is similar to that for a forehand or backhand stroke.

The pinch kill is ideal for the beginning player because he/she can make a mistake in hitting this shot and still score a point. Since the rebound is to a front-court position, even a ball hit too high or one that rebounds off the floor may be impossible for your opponent to reach as long as he/she is in the back court.

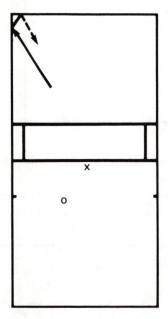 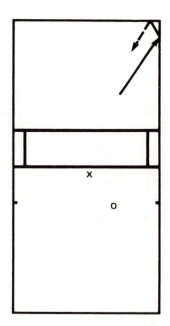

Pinch kill hit away from opponent.

Pinch kill hit to opponent's backhand.

Overhead Kill

The overhead kill shot is popular with beginning players but falls out of favor as the player develops other offensive weapons. The object of the overhead kill is the same as for any kill shot, but the stroking technique is different. This kill shot is hit off a ball that is above shoulder level rather than close to the ground. It is hit from the forehand side with much the same motion used in a tennis serve. The stroke is begun by pivoting and pulling the racquet back as if to hit a forehand stroke (see page 20). However, as the foreward swing is begun, the racquet is lifted in a circular motion as if you were going to throw it to the front wall. The chest and hips are rotated to face the front wall as you step forward to hit the ball. The ball is contacted just in front of the forward foot with an extended arm. At contact, the face of the racquet should be parallel to the front wall. To assume this position, a Western grip is preferred over any other forehand grip to turn the face of the racquet. To maximize the power of the stroke, the ball should always be hit with the arm in an extended position and the stroke completed with a follow-through, dropping the racquet across the body. Ideally, the ball should be directed low into a front corner of

Sequence of overhead kill shot.

the court. To have the best chance of success, the overhead kill should hit a side wall as well as the front wall to deaden the rebound of the ball. Otherwise, if not hit perfectly, the ball will rebound high into the air at the same angle at which it hit the wall. The high bounce gives even a slow opponent adequate time to position him/herself for the return. Consequently, the overhead kill is considered a "low-percentage" shot because it is hard to score a point off a ball that is not hit perfectly. Therefore, beginning players are advised to be patient and wait for the ball to drop below waist level. Then, a corner or pinch kill can be hit. Both of these kill shots are more difficult to return than the overhead kill, even if all shots are hit incorrectly.

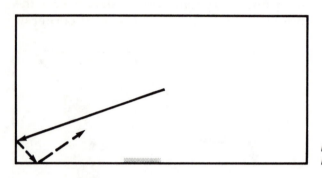

Rebound of overhead kill bouncing high off the floor.

Points to Remember:

1. To be effective, kill shots should combine a low ball hit to the front wall with a forceful stroke and sharp wrist snap.
2. To hit a good kill shot, wait for the ball to fall low to the ground — at least below your knee.
3. When hitting a kill shot, bend your knees and drop your waist to lower your racquet arm to the ground.
4. To hit a level kill shot, keep your racquet face perpendicular to the floor, and swing level with the floor.
5. To direct a kill shot to a front corner, you must angle your racquet face to the corner that you wish to hit.
6. Always angle your kill shot away from your opponent's court position to insure a successful shot.

Passing Shots

A passing shot, unlike the kill shot, requires no new techniques to master. Its effectiveness depends only on your opponent's court position and your ability to place the ball. The passing shot, as its name implies, is a ball that literally goes "past" the opponent.

Therefore, it is most advantageous when the opposing player is in the front-, mid-, or center-court areas. In this way, the ball can go "past" the opponent and "beat" him/her into the back court. If hit

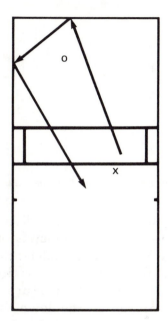

Passing shot hit to opponent in front court.

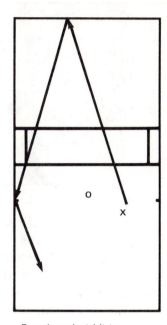

Passing shot hit to opponent in center court.

low off the front wall, a passing shot will die in the back court and not rebound into a center-court position. Without rebounding hard off the back wall, the ball in essence is "out-of-play" except to a heroic effort. At the very least, if the ball is returned, it will usually be a desperation shot that you can return for a winner or at least will push your opponent to use up his/her energy reserves.

The most critical error made by beginning players when using a passing shot is hitting the ball with too much force. As a result, instead of dying in the back court, the ball rebounds off the back wall into play and negates the advantage that the passing shot offers.

The passing shot can be hit with either a forehand, backhand, or overhead stroke. The ball should be directed to hit the front wall at a point between waist and knee height off the floor. In all cases, however, the lower the rebound off the front wall, the less chance that a return will be made. The ball can either be hit directly to a back corner or angled to rebound from the front wall to contact a side wall on the way to the back court. If the ball is angled toward a side wall, it should hit either at the same distance or farther from the front wall as your opponent is standing. This will help not only

Passing shot using the side wall.

to slow the movement of the ball into the back court but discourage your opponent from trying to hit the ball as it rebounds off the front wall because it will be out of reach. Should the ball hit the side wall in front of your opponent's court position, it will pass through the center court and allow your opponent to make a return shot.

Two types of passing shots are common — the down-the-line pass and the cross-court pass.

Down-The-Line Pass

The down-the-line pass could really be called the down-the-wall (wallpaper) pass. This ball is hit so that it travels in a line along the side wall, 1 to 3 feet from it and below waist level. As stated before, hitting the ball too hard will cause a strong rebound off the

Down-the-line pass.

back wall and possibly allow a return to be made. This passing shot is ideally hit when you are between your opponent and the side wall down which you are hitting or when the opposing player is "caught" in a front-court position. In either case, hit the ball toward the side wall that is the farthest distance from your opponent. If he/she is playing a center-court position, hit to the backhand side. A forehand stroke should be used to hit passing shots to the forehand side of the court and a backhand stroke for balls directed to the backhand side.

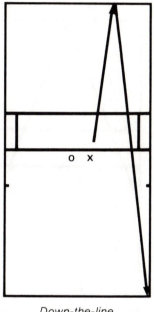

Down-the-line pass

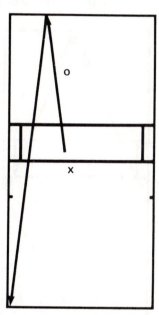

Passing shot when opponent is in front court

Cross-Court Pass

The cross-court pass moves the ball from one side of the court to the other in order to "pass" the opponent. It does this by following the path of a "V" across the court. Dependent upon where you are positioned in the court, the ball will rebound off the front wall close to its center. You must experiment with the exact placement of the ball as you hit from different court positions. What will always be true is that the ball will rebound from the front wall at an angle equal to the angle of impact. To prevent the opponent from hitting the rebound off the front wall, this angle must be large enough to avoid the opponent's reach.

As with a down-the-line pass, the cross-court shot may be hit with a forehand, backhand, or overhead stroke. It is ideally used when your opponent is on your side of the court, is in a center-court position, or is positioned closer to the front wall. One advantage of the passing shot is that it can be hit from anyplace on the court, including the back court, since the success of the shot depends more on your opponent's court position. It is an easy shot to learn and win with because most right-handed players can use their stronger forehands to hit cross-court passing shots to their opponent's weaker backhands.

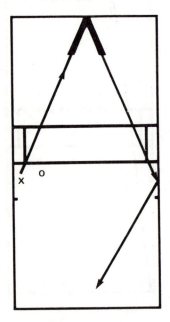
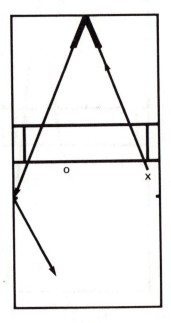

Cross court passing shot with opponent close to side wall.

Cross court passing shot with opponent in center court.

As with a down-the-line pass, a ball that rebounds low into the back court has the greatest chance of success. This ball may also hit a side wall before rebounding into the back-court area. As stated earlier, however, care must be taken to insure that the ball does not rebound through a center-court position or in front of the opponent. Hitting a side wall will also help to slow the speed of the ball on the court, allowing you to hit the ball with more force and still have a successful passing shot.

Since a wide margin of error exists with how hard and at what angle the ball should be hit, successful cross-court passing shots can be made by even the most beginning player.

Points to Remember:

1. A passing shot can be hit with any stroke. Its success is dependent upon your opponent's court position.
2. Do not use a passing shot when your opponent is in a back-court position.
3. A passing shot can be hit cross-court or down-the-line from anyplace on the court.
4. The lower the passing shot rebounds off the front wall, the greater its chance of being a winning shot.
5. The passing shot may hit a side wall after rebounding from the front wall, but it should not be angled to hit in front of the opponent or through the center-court area.
6. Hitting the passing shot too hard will cause the ball to rebound off the back wall into play.

Common Errors and How to Correct Them

1. My kill shots always hit the floor before they reach the front wall.
   A. Usually you have angled the racquet face down at the point of impact with the ball, thus driving the ball into the ground. Concentrate on keeping your racquet face perpendicular to the floor and the stroke parallel to the floor.
2. My kill shots are never low enough to the front wall.
   A. Be patient and wait for the ball to drop closer to the ground before hitting it. This means that you will have to bend your knees and lower your waist to drop your racquet to the ball. Try to make contact with the ball just off the tops of your shoes. If this does not help, you may be scooping at the ball with the racquet and hitting it on the upswing, which lifts the ball to the front wall higher than you want it to hit. A level swing with the floor will correct this problem.
3. I hit my cross-court shots right back to my opponent because the ball bounces off a side wall into the center court.
   A. Take some angle off your hit and aim more for the center of the front wall.

Common Errors and How to Correct Them (Cont.)

4. My down-the-line passing shot always hits the side wall.

    A. Your racquet head is not parallel to the front wall when you contact the ball, but is angled toward the side wall that you are hitting. Hold the wrist stiff and swing through the ball. Also, check to make sure that you are contacting the ball off your forward foot. Contacting the ball in front of or behind this position will cause the ball to rebound at an angle off the front wall.

5. My overhead kill shot hits (a) the floor first or (b) too high off the front wall.

    A. (a) When the floor is hit first, either the ball is hit when it is too far in front of you or when your wrist is bent too much, causing the racquet head to be angled to the floor. Check the position of your body relative to the ball when you hit the overhead, and hold the racquet so that it appears to be an extension of your arm.

    (b) Hitting the ball too high off the front wall usually results from hitting the ball too far behind your front foot or even over your head, which prohibits you from angling the hit downward. Again, check the position of the ball when you make contact, and be sure that the contact point is in front of your forward foot.

6. My passing shots always rebound off the back wall into a center-court position.

    A. Take some of the force off your stroke, and hit the ball lower off the front wall to insure a shorter rebound from the back. If this does not help, try to hit a side wall to deaden the ball's movement.

Chapter Four

Defensive Strokes

Rather than scoring a point, the purpose of a defensive shot is to PREVENT your opponent from hitting a winning shot. This goal can be achieved only if the ball rebounds high off the front wall, preventing a kill-shot return, or rebounds to a court position that provides little space from which to hit an offensive return. Ideally, the best defensive shot is hit in such a way as to have the ball rebound from the front wall high into the back court and close to the side wall. Several strokes accomplish this purpose, at least one of which should immediately be in your repertoire of shots.

Ceiling Shot (Front Wall-Ceiling)

This ceiling shot can be hit with a forehand or backhand stroke off a ball that falls below waist level or with an overhand stroke on a high ball. A front-wall-to-ceiling shot hits the front wall before the ceiling. Upon contact with the front wall, the ball rebounds to the ceiling close to the front wall-ceiling crotch and then is directed downward to bounce on the floor just past the short line. If hit with enough force, the rebound of the ball off the floor will carry the ball high over the head of the opponent and into a back corner, dying upon impact with the back corner. Since the ball must be returned before striking the floor twice, your opponent must hit the ball from this corner position without the benefit of a rebound off the

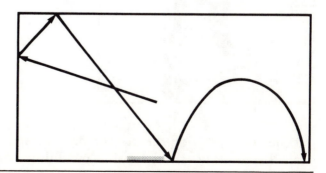

Front wall - Ceiling shot.

floor. Thus, this court position makes it difficult to hit an offensive shot because of the ball's proximity to the walls. However, the harder you hit a front wall-ceiling shot, the higher the height of the bounce off the floor and the greater the chance the ball will hit and rebound off the back wall with enough force to provide room to hit the ball before it touches the floor. Therefore, care must be taken to hit the ball with adequate force to provide a high bounce to force the opponent to the back corner but not so hard as to cause a rebound off the back wall into a center-court position.

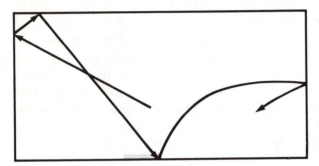

Front wall - Ceiling hit with too much force and rebounding off the back wall.

The front wall-ceiling shot hit from a ball that has dropped below waist level begins as any other forehand or backhand stroke. The pivot to the side wall is followed by the backswing with the wrist cocked. However, as the forward swing is begun, the racquet head must be turned back, or "opened," toward the ceiling. This

Open racquet for ceiling shot.

racquet face position directs the ball toward the top of the front wall. In addition, the use of a pendulum, or "scooping" swing, instead of a stroke that is parallel to the floor, will help to "lift" the ball to the height needed.

Pendulum swing.

The front wall-ceiling shot hit with an overhead stroke, whether from the forehand or backhand side, is similar in technique to an overhead kill shot (see page 38). Like the kill shot, contact with the ball is made just off the forward foot, with the hips and chest facing the front wall and the arm extended. A Western grip is preferred by many players, since it opens the face of the racquet to the ceiling. The difference between the ceiling shot and the offensive kill return is the angle of the racquet face when the ball is

Backhand overhead ceiling shot *(continued on page 50)*

contacted. The face must be angled toward the top of the front wall. To do this, the wrist cannot be snapped from its laid-back position on the forward swing. This will keep the racquet directed upward. The stroke should finish with a follow-through to insure hitting the ball with power.

Laid back racquet for overhead ceiling shot.

A front wall-ceiling shot is most effective if hit when your opponent is already in the back court. The ball strikes the floor close to the short line, which means that if your opponent is playing nearby, he/she may be tempted to hit the ball immediately after the bounce. A back-court position would not result in the same temptation, and the desired effect of the ceiling shot can be achieved.

To insure the most difficult return possible, the front wall-ceiling shot should be directed to "run" along a side wall before it bounces into the back corner. If in addition the ball is directed to your opponent's backhand side, this defensive shot may not only result in a weak return but possibly no return at all. Thus, this defensive shot may actually score a point for you.

Ceiling Shot (Ceiling-Front Wall Shot)

A variation of the front wall-ceiling shot is one that hits both walls but in the reverse order. Although both ceiling shots are hit with a similar technique, this ceiling shot is hit with a racquet that is angled more toward the ceiling. The ball should be directed to hit the ceiling approximately 2 to 3 feet from the ceiling/front wall crotch. With this stroke, the ball will rebound to the floor, hitting in front of the service zone before bouncing into the back-court area.

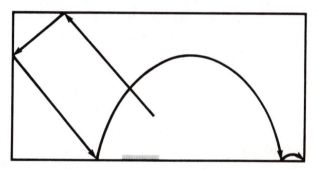

Ceiling - front wall
defensive shot.

The advantage of a ceiling-front wall shot is that it can be an effective defensive shot even if your opponent is near center court. The ball rebounds to the floor in front of the service line, which means that your opponent must retreat to the back court to await the fall of the ball. Thus, with this shot the opponent will be forced into a poor court position. In all other respects, the strategic use of a ceiling-front wall shot is the same as for a front wall-ceiling shot: (1) keep the ball in play; (2) move your opponent to a back-court position; and (3) force a return that is not an offensive shot.

Either ceiling shot can be hit from any part of the court and should be practiced from all court positions. If you are standing to one side of center, you can hit the shot down the closest side wall (wallpaper shot) or hit cross-court to the opposite corner. The cross-court ceiling shot requires more power in the stroke because of the diagonal court distance to be covered as well as the need for accurate placement. If the ball is not hit at a sharp angle, the rebound forward will be away from the side wall and will provide for easy stroking room. A similar problem exists with a ceiling shot hit down-the-line if it does not "hug" the wall. Thus, although the ceiling shot is one of the easiest defensive strokes to learn, unless time is taken to practice placement, the true advantage of the shot cannot be achieved.

Points to Remember:

1. When the ball hits the racquet, the angle of the racquet head must be directed to the spot on the front wall or ceiling that you want the ball to hit.
2. To hit a ceiling shot from a ball below waist level, open the racquet face and use a pendulum swing.
3. Ceiling shots hit with an overhead stroke should contact the ball in front of the forward foot with an extended arm.
4. Angle all ceiling shots so that they rebound into a back corner, preferably to your opponent's backhand.
5. Hitting a ceiling shot with too much force can result in the ball rebounding off the back wall and into play.

Lob Shot

A lob shot is not played as often in competitive racquetball as other defensive shots. This is due to the popularity of the composite/graphite racquets and the use of pressurized balls. The lob is a shot that requires finesse and placement, not the power and strength for which this equipment was designed. Therefore, players that choose a fast-moving, power game often do not have the finesse necessary to hit a lob return.

A lob is struck with a technique similar to a ceiling shot hit from a ball falling below waist level. Both shots, whether hit with a forehand or backhand stroke, require a pendulum forward swing. Contact with the ball should be made with an extended arm and open face racquet off the forward foot. Although not much force is required to hit this ball properly, the ball should be struck with your weight shifted toward the front wall. Finish the stroke with a follow-through high over your head. This arm motion and the racquet face angle serve to "lift" the ball.

Like the ceiling shot, the lob is returned high to the front wall, approximately 6 to 8 feet from the ceiling. However, the lob shot

Backhand lob shot.

differs from the ceiling shot in that the ball never rebounds to touch the ceiling. Rather, the ball slowly moves along a line close to the ceiling and high over center court, falling "dead" into a back corner with little or no rebound from the back wall. When perfectly hit, the slow movement of this ball allows you time to reposition yourself on the court, yet forces your opponent into the disadvantages of a back-corner return.

Similar to the ceiling shot, a lob may be hit down-the-line or cross-court. If the lob is hit down-the-line, it is preferable to use a backhand shot down the left side wall and a forehand shot to the right side wall for more control. A cross-court lob may be hit with

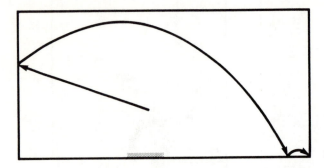

Lob defensive shot.

either stroke. The purpose of both shots is to place the ball in a back-court position to prevent an offensive return. Thus, the lob presents many of the same problems to your opponent as the ceiling shot does. The reason why it is not hit more often is because it is a difficult shot to hit correctly. Since the ball does not rebound from the ceiling on the way to the back court, the ball, if hit too hard, will merely rebound off the back wall into a center-court position. Thus,

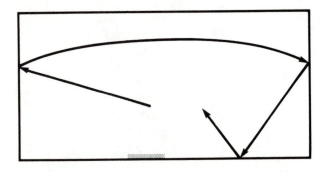

Lob shot rebounding into center court off the back wall.

the advantage of a back-corner placement is lost. In addition, because the ball moves so slowly, it is easy to hit a strong return unless the lob is placed correctly. To minimize any possible rebound off the back wall, aim the lob so that the ball just brushes against a side wall. This "meeting" will slow the ball and deaden its fall to the floor. For most beginners, the finesse with which this ball must be hit is hard to manage in a game situation where quick movements are necessary. Yet, the lob does offer an interesting variation for the player who can use it, including changing the pace of the game.

Points to Remember:

1. Remember to pivot the hips and use a pendulum swing with an open racquet face to hit the ball.

2. Hit the ball as hard as you think necessary, then take some force off your swing.
3. Finish the stroke with a follow-through, with the racquet ending up high over your shoulder.
4. To take some power out of your shot, aim the ball to "brush" the side wall close to the back corner.
5. To be more effective, lob only to a back corner.

High Z-Ball or Three-Wall Shot

Like the other defensive shots, the high Z or three-wall shot is designed to move the opponent into a back corner. The high Z can be hit with either an overhead stroke from a high ball or a stroke using a pendulum motion on a waist-level return. To insure proper placement of the ball, the racquet head at contact must again be angled in the direction toward which the ball should travel. This means that the racquet face should be slightly open. In all other respects, the high Z stroke also resembles one of the other defensive shots. The overhead stroke is similar to the overhead ceiling shot (see page 49, while the high Z, hit from a waist-level ball, is similar to the lob (see page 52).

As in other defensive shots, the high Z must be directed to hit high off the front wall and close to a ceiling crotch (3 to 4 feet from it). However, a high Z differs from other defensive shots in that the ball moves diagonally across the court to the back wall. In essence, the movement of the ball describes a "Z" through the court. To follow this path, the ball must hit the front wall not only high, but within 3 to 4 feet of a front corner crotch. After contact with the front wall, the ball hits the closest side wall and rebounds to follow the long diagonal of the court to a back corner position, hitting the back wall.

The placement of the ball on the front wall is critical to the effectiveness of this shot. If hit too low, the Z ball is an easy setup for your opponent. This is because the ball passes over a center-court position when following the diagonal. A ball hit too low will pass through the center court area within arm's reach of your opponent. As long as the ball is hit high off the front wall, it will pass high over the center court and force your opponent into a back-court position to return the ball.

Depending upon the strength of the hit, the Z ball may or may not hit a second side wall before touching the floor in the back

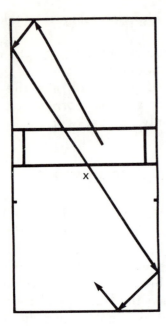
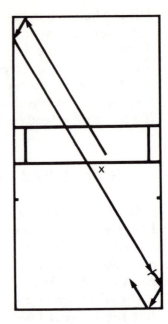

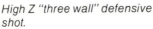

High Z "three wall" defensive shot.

High Z defensive shot hitting floor before back corner.

corner. If hit hard, a second wall will be hit on the opposite side from the first before the ball rebounds to the floor. Thus, the name "three"-wall is often used to identify this shot. In this situation, the ball will "run the corner" by hitting the side wall, the back wall, and then the floor in succession.

Because the ball "covers" so much of the court on a Z-ball return, women and beginning level playes often do not have a powerful enough stroke to hit the shot well. It is good to practice this shot often and feel confident about hitting it before trying a Z-ball return in a game situation.

Although a Z ball may be hit from anywhere in the court, you should try it from a center-court position if your shot is weak. Stronger players will be effective with a high Z hit even from the back court. Because of the path followed by the ball, the Z is best hit to the opposite corner from your court position. Otherwise, the angle off the front wall will not be great enough to cause a rebound along the diagonal.

The Z-ball or three-wall shot is very effective in causing a weak return, especially if the ball "runs the corner." In the back corner, there is little room to place a racquet and stroke through the ball unless timing is perfect and a good wrist snap is used. Therefore, this shot is often hit by more experienced players not only to force a bad court position on the opponent, but to "handcuff" him/her as well.

Points to Remember:

1. Hit the ball high off the front wall and close to the side wall/front wall crotch.
2. Use a stroke similar to an overhead ceiling shot for balls over your shoulder and a lob return for waist-high balls.
3. Hit the ball hard enough to "run the corner" of the back court.
4. Hit the high Z to the corner opposite from the side of the court in which you are positioned.

Common Errors and How to Correct Them

1. My ceiling shots never hit the ceiling.
   A. If the ball is hit from a position below the waist, you are not "scooping" or hitting underneath the ball to lift it high enough to hit the front wall and/or ceiling. If you are using an overhead stroke, the ball is probably too far in front of you when you contact it, or your racquet head is not angled toward the ceiling to direct the ball upward.
2. My ceiling shots hit the ceiling straight over my head.
   A. For both waist-level and overhead shots, you have angled your racquet too much, and the racquet face is almost parallel to the ceiling. In addition, with the overhead stroke, the ball is probably contacted over your head rather than in front of your forward foot.
3. My ceiling shots rebound off the back wall into the playing area.
   A. You are hitting the ball too hard or with too little angle off the front wall. Aim closer to the front wall-ceiling crotch, and ease the force of your stroke.
4. My lob always hits the ceiling.
   A. You have too much force in your hit and/or too much angle on the racquet head. Hit the ball softer, and aim for a point lower on the front wall.

(Continued on page 58)

Common Errors and How to Correct Them (Cont.)

5. My lob always hits the back wall and rebounds to center court.
   A. Try to angle the hit more into the back corner of the court, then limit the force with which the ball is hit. If the ball does rebound into the court, it will at least be along the wall and will still provide little stroking room.

6. My high Z does not hit the back wall corner but goes straight into the back wall.
   A. Angle your hit into the front wall closer to the front wall-side wall crotch by changing the direction of the racquet head.

7. My high Z bounces too high off the back wall and gives my opponent an easy return.
   A. Hit the ball lower to the front wall, or softer and with more of an upward stroking motion so that the ball arches into the back court.

8. My high Z ball always rebounds off the front wall-side wall and bounces at center court, where it is returned by my opponent.
   A. Make sure that you are pivoting your hips before you stroke and that you are stepping into the ball. If you rely only on the strength of your arm to hit the ball, the force may not be great enough and the ball may not complete the diagonal of the court before touching the court floor.

Chapter Five

Serves in Racquetball

Serving is the most important offensive weapon in the arsenal of a beginning player. For the intermediate player, the serve either "sets" up a winning shot or prevents the opponent from scoring on the return of serve. The effectiveness of the serve is due to the controlled way in which it can be hit. This is the only time when contact with the ball is made at a predetermined location. Thus, you can play to your strengths and your opponent's weaknesses if you can consistently serve your best shot.

There are only five basic serves. Each serve, however, can be changed to give a slightly different look by varying the power with which it is hit, its height of rebound off the front wall, and the angle of rebound into the back court. With these variations, the basic serves can become hundreds of different shots. The wise player mixes these variations to keep his/her opponent guessing as to "where" the next ball will be served. However, the serve chosen should only be hit after thought is given to an opponent's strengths and skills. Even a well-placed serve, if hit so that an opponent can return it with his/her favorite shot, is nothing more than a nice "setup." Similarly, a good player never hits a weak serve merely for the sake of variety if he/she is not sure that an equally weak return will follow.

For an opponent who you have never seen play, a good strategy is simply to serve to his/her backhand with your best serve. If a player has a weakness, it is usually on the backhand side, and at least this strategy will increase the odds of your winning the point with your serve.

Most important, in order to make these variations effective, your serve must not become predictable, either in the position that you take in the service court or in the technique with which you strike the ball. Ideally, all serves should be hit from a similar position on the court, with a similar stroke. Usually a center-court position and normal forehand stroke are used. In this way, it is difficult, if

Serving position on the court.

not impossible, for your opponent to anticipate the positioning of your serve. This means that variation in your serve must be a result of the amount of wrist snap or the position of the racquet face at the moment of contact with the ball. Either factor will affect the angle of hit or the power of the stroke.

Since you as the server are the only one who knows where the serve will be hit, you should also anticipate the placement of the returned ball. So take the time before each serve to not only plan the best serve, but the most likely return and how best to play the ball. Ideally, if the serve is not an outright winner, at least a poor return should occur, setting you up for your best offensive stroke.

The serve provides the server with the offensive advantage in the game. To serve without purpose or thought to your opponent's skill gives up this advantage and possibly the serve with it.

Legal Serves

For a serve to be legal, a ball is hit after it rebounds off the floor within the service zone. After contact with the racquet, the ball must strike the front wall before any other part of the court. However, the rebounding ball from the front wall may touch one side wall before falling to the floor behind the short line. The ball may not touch the floor in front of the short line (short), a second side wall (two-wall), the ceiling (ceiling), or back wall (long) before the ball falls to the floor. A two-wall, short, long, or ceiling serve is a fault and should not be played.

Most serves are hit with a forehand stroke. The server stands as far back as possible in the service zone with his/her hips pivoted to the side wall. Ideally, both feet should be placed along the short line. This provides as much service zone as possible in which to step forward when contacting the ball. Stepping out of the service zone during the serve is illegal.

To begin the serve, the ball rolls off the fingertips of the open hand and is dropped to the floor. The arm should be extended to the front wall so that the ball is dropped as far forward in the service zone as possible. If the ball is not dropped close to the service line,

Foot placement to begin serve.

Ball drop for service.

the server will move past the ball when stepping forward to hit it. Thus, contact with the ball will occur behind the forward foot, and much of the force of the stroke will be lost.

At the beginning of the serve, the racquet has already completed the backswing and is held perpendicular to the back wall. When the ball leaves the hand, the forward swing of the racquet begins. The type of swing used (level or pendulum) and the height of the ball off the floor at contact are dependent upon the serve being hit. In any serve, however, it is essential to step into the stroke. The shifting of the body's weight from the back of the service zone to the foot that steps toward the service line provides additional power.

The serve, as any other stroke, is completed with a follow-through, the final position of the racquet being dependent upon the type of serve used. It is important to always hit "through" the ball rather than merely "punch" at it if a strong serve is desired.

Although most serves are hit with a forehand stroke, on occasion a backhand or overhead stroke may be used.

The following five serves are designed to follow the rules of service as well as place the opponent in a poor court position from which to hit an offensive return. As described with defensive strokes, this means hitting a ball into a back corner of the court. On all serves, it is important to keep the ball in the back corners and away from the midline of the court. A return from the middle of the court provides too many opportunities for offensive shots and prevents the server from holding a center-court position. Thus, the following serves should be directed wide of the midline of the court and should only rebound back to a center-court position after bouncing twice on the floor and being ruled a dead ball!

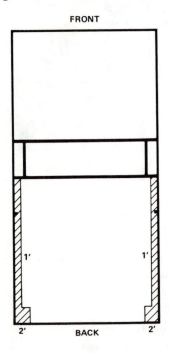

Court areas for served ball to be directed.

Lob

The lob serve is hit identically to the lob defensive shot, with the ball following the same path through the court (see page 54). The serve may be hit cross-court or down-the-line. As in the defensive lob, the ball must be hit high to the front wall, and the rebound should arch its way high over center court to die in a back-court corner. To do this, the forward swing of the stroke must involve a pendulum motion, with the racquet face slightly open to the ceiling. The ball is hit below waist level and lifted to the point of contact with the front wall. The stroke is finished with the racquet held high over the forward shoulder. As in the defensive lob, a lob serve requires finesse rather than power.

Lob Serve.

To insure that the ball will die in the back court, the lob serve can graze a side wall close to the back wall. This rebound will slow the movement of the ball. As a result, the serve must be accurately directed to a corner. Accuracy in placement is critical. If the ball does not "handcuff" your opponent in the back corner, this slow-moving ball will be an easy setup for an offensive return. If this is difficult for you to do, hit the serve to the opponent's backhand. This will provide for a margin of error in placement because it will force a weak-side return.

To increase the accuracy of the lob serve to the backhand side of the court, many players will change their center-court serving position and move to that side of the service zone. In addition, they will hit the ball with a backhand stroke using the same pendulum swing and open racquet face as on the forehand side. Although there is little deception in this maneuver, the difficulty in returning a lob serve comes not in surprising the opponent as much as in placing the ball. This court position allows for better placement because the ball is not hit at an angle. Rather, the racquet head is parallel to the front wall and the ball is hit straight.

The lob is a good serve to use to change the pace of the game and to slow down a fast-moving opponent who likes to return serves hard to the front wall. The lob can be varied by hitting the serve at a "half lob" position, i.e., one which is about shoulder height at the peak of its arch. Again, accuracy of placement is critical in the success of this serve.

Drive Serve

A drive serve is hit with a strong forehand stroke, as it is the hardest serve hit. To maximize the power in the stroke, it is essential that you turn your hips sideways to the front wall and that you meet the ball by stepping into it during the forward swing. The ball should be contacted low in relation to the body — somewhere between the bent knee and the ankle. The forward swing should be level to the ground and the ball met just in front of the forward foot. The follow-through should be low to the ground and should pull the shoulders around to finish the stroke facing the front wall. This serve resembles the kill shot in technique.

To be most effective, the drive serve should be hit low to the front wall to insure a low ball rebounding into the back court. Keeping the ball low adds to the difficulty in the return.

There is not one particular area of the court to which the drive serve should be directed. As in other serves, however, the serve should not be hit close to the midline of the back court. The ball can hit the side wall just past the short line (short corner drive serve), go straight into the back corner of the court, or hit the side wall several feet from the back wall and rebound "around the back corner." Any of these serves will be effective as long as you vary the

Drive serve.

angle of rebound off the front wall from serve to serve and keep the ball low. To do this, the angle of the racquet face at ball contact must change with each hit. To prevent your opponent from anticipating the position of your serve, learn to hit a drive serve to the forehand and backhand sides of the court with equal skill. However, the backhand side is most effective in preventing offensive returns.

If your opponent "moves up" on your drive serve to take the ball before it touches the ground, hit the ball with more angle to the side wall. This will direct the ball farther back into the court and avoid your opponent's reach.

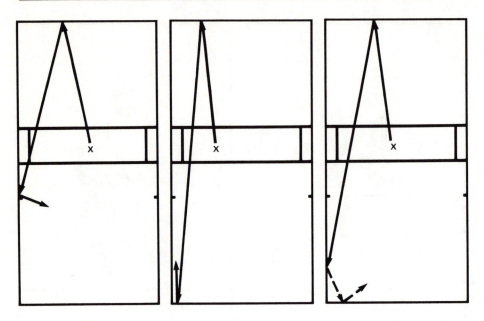

Variations of drive serves: behind short line, to back corner and off side wall.

Z Serve

The Z serve can be divided into two distinct serves — a high Z serve and a low Z serve. The high Z serve is similar to the defensive Z shot in its movement around the court. This serve hits high on the front wall close to the front wall-side wall crotch. The ball rebounds to the nearest side wall, then travels high across the

High Z serve.

diagonal of the court to the opposite back corner. For the serve to be legal, however, the ball must hit the floor before touching another wall (unlike the defensive Z shot) and rebounding again. Thus, the movement of the ball on the court resembles the letter "Z".

This Z serve is hit with the same technique as the defensive Z shot (see page 55). The hips are turned to the side wall, and the forward swing follows a pendulum motion. The racquet face is open, and contact with the ball is made in front of the forward foot. However, the stroke cannot be as strong as the defensive shot because the ball must touch the floor before the opposite side wall is struck. Thus, like the lob serve, the high Z serve needs proper placement and finesse, rather than power, to be effective.

On the opposite extreme, the low Z ball requires power to make the shot work. The low Z serve follows the same "Z" path around the court, but instead of travelling above shoulder height, the ball moves through the court close to the ground. Thus, this serve is hit low to the front wall, similar to the drive serve but with more strength because of the distance across the court that the ball must travel before touching the floor.

The technique used to hit a low Z serve is similar to that for a kill shot (see page 31). The ball must be contacted in front of the forward foot as the weight is shifted forward. The racquet should have a level swing at contact with the ball, and the arm movement must be completed with a follow-through. "Punching" at the ball by stopping the racquet's motion after hitting the ball will only limit the power of the swing. A good wrist snap is also essential in providing the power necessary to hit a low Z ball.

Low Z serve.

The low Z may rebound to the floor anywhere along the side wall past the short line. If the ball is hit hard and close to the front wall-side wall crotch, the ball will rebound to the floor just behind the short line and hit the side wall. The extreme spin on the ball, due to the power of the stroke, will cause the ball to rebound almost straight off the side wall. Thus, an opponent positioned to hit a ball served deep into a back corner will be out of place to return this serve.

If the ball is hit several feet from the front wall-side wall crotch, the ball will be directed toward the back corner of the court. The different angles that can be used to hit the low Z serve depend on the angle of the racquet head when the ball is contacted. The variety of angles provides another means of preventing your opponent from knowing where to set up for the return of serve.

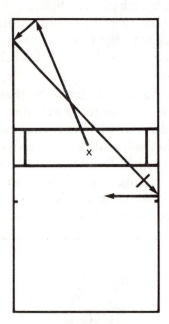

Low Z serve hitting past short line.

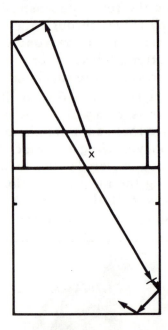

Low Z serve directed to the back corner of the court.

To be most successful, however, the low Z ball requires a powerful and accurate stroke. If the ball is moving too slowly, the opponent may be tempted to hit the ball as it passes through the center-court position. For this reason, the low Z ball is used primarily by experienced players and seldom by beginning players who have not mastered shifting their body weight and snapping the wrist to increase the power of the serve. Beginning players rely on the high Z serve, hit with the pendulum stroke. Although this serve results in a slow-moving ball, it can be especially effective if hit to the backhand of a hard-hitting opponent because it is placed into a back corner.

Overhead Serve

The overhead serve is rarely used in competitive racquetball, but it is a legal serve. It is hit with a stroke similar to that used in an overhead kill, but the ball is not directed as low to the front wall as in the kill shot. The most difficult part of the stroke is starting the ball in play, since the ball must be hit only after rebounding off the floor. Therefore, to be contacted at a point over your head, the ball must hit the floor of the service area with enough force so that it rebounds above your head and outstretched arm. Thus, the ball must be "thrown" to the floor rather than dropped. Because this throw must be done with your non-racquet, i.e., non-dominant hand, the throw is a difficult one to make. If the ball is not thrown straight down, it will rebound out of the service area rather than overhead and cannot be hit. If the ball is not thrown with enough force, it will not bounce high enough for a proper overhead stroke. Therefore, if you anticipate using an overhead serve in a game, the throw should be practiced until its placement is consistent. If the throw is done correctly, the overhead stroke should contact the ball just in front of the forward foot with the racquet held in an extended arm.

To hit the ball with the most control, the server should use a Western grip. The backswing and forward swing of the stroke resembles a circle, much like a tennis serve. The ball should be contacted at a point overhead after you have stepped onto your forward foot and shifted your body weight forward onto the ball of this foot. Until the point of impact, the racquet face should trail the wrist. Upon contact with the ball, the wrist and racquet should be snapped forward to direct the ball toward the bottom third of the front wall. This "snapping" will not only direct the ball downward, but increase the force of the stroke. The overhead serve is completed with a follow-through that brings the racquet downward across the body.

The ball should hit the front wall 3 to 5 feet off the floor. This will insure a low rebound into the back court. If the serve is hit lower, the ball will hit the floor in front of the short line and be

Overhead serve.

called a fault. This is due to the sharp downward angle of the stroke. To rebound into a back corner, the ball must contact the front wall at least 1 foot on either side of the center when you are serving from the middle of the service zone. The overhead serve offers no unique advantage except a "different" look. Some beginning players like to hit an overhead serve because of its similarity to a tennis serve, with which they are familiar and can hit with power. However, the most difficult serves to return are not necessarily the most powerful, but rather those that are most accurately placed and rebound low into a back-corner position. Because the ball is hit down to the front wall with an overhead serve, the ball will often rebound off the floor with a high bounce. Thus, the ball may not be close to the floor in the back court. Therefore, keeping the ball low to the floor on the serve as done with the drive or low Z is more effective. This is why these serves are preferred by experienced players.

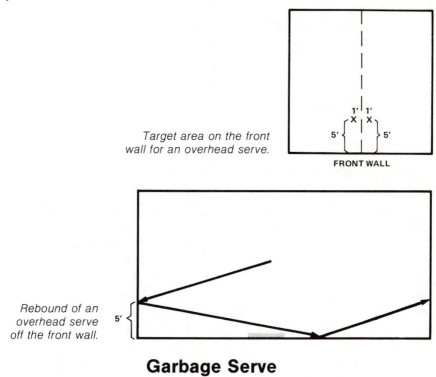

Target area on the front wall for an overhead serve.

FRONT WALL

Rebound of an overhead serve off the front wall.

Garbage Serve

A garbage serve is hit with a forehand stroke. This serve "looks" much like a drive serve. The forward swing is level to the floor, and the ball is contacted off the front foot. The force of the hit is dependent upon the speed of the swing and the snap of the wrist when the ball is contacted. The ball should not be hit as hard as it is in a drive serve, nor as softly as in the lob. Yet, the follow-through should draw the racquet across the body to hit "through" the ball. However, the movement of the ball on the court gives the impresion that the ball has been mis-hit. Although the ball should rebound wide of the midline of the court, it is not hit low to the floor or high to the ceiling. Rather, the ball rebounds into the back court at a height between waist and shoulder level off the floor. To hit the ball to this height, the serve must contact the ball at a point higher off the floor than for a drive serve or with the racquet face slightly open.

This serve may or may not be hit with enough angle to rebound off a side wall before entering the back court. If it is, the ball should

Garbage serve to back corner.

just brush the back wall so that the ball does not rebound back into play. In this respect, a garbage serve is similar to a half-lob.

If the serve is directed straight into the back corner, the ball must not be hit hard enough to rebound strongly off the back wall. A strong rebound at this point will negate the value of the garbage serve. The strategy behind this serve is to force a ceiling return and/or prevent your opponent from hitting a kill shot or other offensive return. This strategy is especially effective with an opponent who can hit offensive shots consistently off your best serve, placing you immediately on the defensive. Using a garbage serve should at least "get" you past the serve and onto other opportunities to win the point.

Points to Remember:

1. Unless a serve requires a different court position, serve from the center of the service zone with a forehand stroke so that you don't "signal" the type of serve you will hit.
2. Never serve the ball down the midline of the court, where an offensive return is easy to hit.
3. In addition to hitting the serve wide of the middle of the court, hit the ball low unless a garbage serve, lob, or high Z is desired.
4. Serve to your opponent's weak side (usually his/her backhand).
5. Practice serving to the right-hand side of the court in case you play a left-handed player (this will be his/her backhand side) and to provide variation in your serve.

6. Practice hitting your serves to rebound at different angles off the front wall, using varying heights off the floor and changing the power in your stroke.

7. The closer to the center of the front wall the ball is hit, the farther back in the court the ball will strike a side wall. The closer to a front-wall corner the ball strikes, the closer to the front wall the ball will hit the side wall.

8. Use a lob or high Z ball to change the pace of the game and/or force a ceiling ball return.

Common Errors and How to Correct Them

1. My lob serve hits the ceiling or the back wall.

    A. You are hitting the ball too hard or with too much angle toward the ceiling. Hit the ball softer and with less angle, i.e., so that the ball hits lower on the front wall.

2. My drive serve rebounds off the back wall into the center court.

    A. Drop your knees closer to the ground so that you can drop your racquet lower to the floor. This will allow you to contact the ball when it is closer to the floor. Hitting a lower ball into the back court will lessen the chance of a rebound off the back wall. In addition, angling the ball to hit a side wall before it touches the back-court floor should "deaden" the movement of the ball into the back court and prevent a hard rebound from the back wall.

3. My Z ball hits two side walls before it hits the floor.

    A. Hit the ball farther from the front corner and closer to the center of the front wall so that the ball will rebound to a point farther into the back court. Another correction would be to hit the ball with less stroking power while keeping the same scooping forward swing to maintain the height of the ball's contact with the front wall.

4. My drive serve "pops" off the front wall and rebounds high into the back court.

    A. You probably are standing up as you make contact with the ball during the serve. If you do not maintain a low position to the floor throughout the forward swing, the ball will be lifted along with your body and rebound up off the front wall. Make sure that you have followed through your serving motion before you come to a ready position to prepare for the return of serve.

(Continued on page 74)

Common Errors and How to Correct Them (Cont.)

5. My garbage serve hits straight into the back wall.

   A. You are hitting the serve too hard. Take some power off your stroke, and angle the racquet head slightly toward the ceiling upon contact with the ball.

6. My serves go straight down the center of the court.

   A. You are not hitting the ball with enough angle (toward a front-wall corner). This can be corrected in one of two ways: (1) Throw the ball out in front of you and toward your backhand side if you want to hit the ball to the side wall behind you. Throw the ball slightly behind the front foot and toward your forehand side if you want to hit the ball toward the side wall that you are facing. (2) Always throw the ball in the same place relative to your body, but concentrate on breaking your wrist upon contact with the ball if you want to serve to the side wall behind you. Open up your wrist (laid back position) if you want to hit toward the side wall that you are facing. This technique is the best because it will disguise your service direction until contact is made.

7. My overhead serve always hits the floor in front of the short line.

   A. You are hitting the ball too low to the front wall. Check to see if you are hitting the ball just in front of your forward foot and if your racquet head is angled in the direction in which you want the ball to go. If so, then you must aim at a higher point off the floor for the ball to contact the front wall. To do this, don't snap your wrist as much when contacting the ball, and/or hit the ball when it is at a higher point on its rebound.

Chapter Six

Use of Back Wall and Corners

Offensive and defensive strokes comprise the major part of the game of racquetball skillwise, but there is also skill involved in playing the court correctly. Use of the walls as an aid to developing your game takes thought and practice.

The Back Wall

Up to now, this book has ignored the part of racquetball that makes it an interesting and challenging game — the use of the back wall. Beginning players often "learn to play" racquetball by avoiding the back wall completely. As a result, they are not really playing four-wall racquetball. This type of play puts these players at a disadvantage when facing an opponent who uses the whole court. Without using the back wall as a playable surface, two problems occur: (1) any ball that gets past your position in the court is a lost ball with no chance for you to retrieve it and (2) in order to prevent balls from going behind you, players use many unorthodox strokes with unpredictable results in returning the ball. Thus, when not using the back wall, players must often resort to merely hitting the ball to keep it in play rather than directing it. This is a strategy that is referred to as "Battleball."

When playing "Battleball," the player maintains a center-court position and hits every ball within his/her reach as hard as possible back to the middle of the front wall — the strategy being, if the ball is hit hard to the front wall, it may rebound past the opponent and score a point. Of course, this tactic may work against another "Battleball" player, but the experienced opponent will skillfully use the back wall to keep the ball in play. Only until you feel confident enough to use the back wall will you be able to play more than "Battleball" on the racquetball court.

The key factor in using the back wall well is PATIENCE — having the patience to let a ball intentionally go past you. Before you can play with "patience," you must develop confidence in your ability to play balls on the rebound off the back wall. Part of this confidence comes from many hours of court practice and another part from an understanding of why the back wall is helpful.

The use of the back wall is important because it provides several advantages during the game. First, a ball that goes past you into the back court can still be hit as it rebounds off the back wall. Second, by waiting for balls to rebound off the back wall, you can move into a better position for hitting a forehand or backhand stroke, i.e., setup for the return. If the ball is hit before the back-wall rebound, often it is above or below the ideal hitting area. It is impossible to practice hitting balls at all positions relative to your body. Thus, always adjusting your court position so that the ball is at the same place relative to your forehand or backhand stroke will insure a consistent hit. This means that you will be in control of the ball's movement around the court and consequently your opponent's court position as well. Finally, waiting for the rebound affords you more time to "see" where your opponent is waiting in the court and to plan the most effective offensive return. Thus, the use of the back wall adds to your ability to control the movement of the ball and your opponent's court position and to potentially gain an offensive advantage.

In order to position yourself to hit a good return off the back wall, you must never lose eye contact with the ball or turn your back to the front wall. The most critical mistake that players make when returning balls off the back wall is turning to face the back

Cross-stepping for back wall return.

wall when stroking the ball. As a result, a normal forehand or backhand stroke cannot be used because the ball would be hit into a side wall. Thus, out of desperation, the player facing the back wall resorts to flipping the ball over his/her shoulder, hitting a blind shot toward the front. This shot does not allow you to control and direct the movement of the ball — only to keep it in play. Thus, the only way to successfully use the back wall is to pivot your hips for a forehand or backhand return and adjust your position relative to the ball's rebound by cross-stepping up or back. The critical decision to be made when returning a ball from the back wall is whether to use a forehand or backhand shot. This decision must be made quickly, and the pivot to the appropriate side should follow immediately. It is easy to judge the side from which most balls should

Watching the ball as it rebounds to back wall.

be hit. However, balls that follow the diagonal of the court are more difficult to play. Usually these balls begin in the front court and end in the back court at opposite corners. Therefore, a ball that begins on your left side becomes a hit from the right side, and you must pivot to the opposite corner from where the ball rebounds in the front court. Practicing moving for these balls on the court is the best way to learn how to position yourself.

To hit any ball off the back wall properly, a player can never afford to take his/her eyes off the ball from the rebound off the front wall to the back-wall hit. Follow the ball from your pivot position, moving only your head to keep the ball in sight.

Once the pivot to the appropriate side has been made, proper positioning for the rebound will either allow you to "make or miss" the shot. It is hard to learn how to adjust your position for the ball without going into the court and practicing. But a few general guidelines may be helpful in getting you started.

If the ball has touched the floor before it hits the back wall, you must hit it before it touches the floor again, i.e., directly off the rebound. Because it has touched the floor, the ball's bounce is deadened and will not rebound far off the back wall. Thus, you will need to move close to the back wall to hit the ball. However, if the ball hits the back wall without touching the floor, you should wait

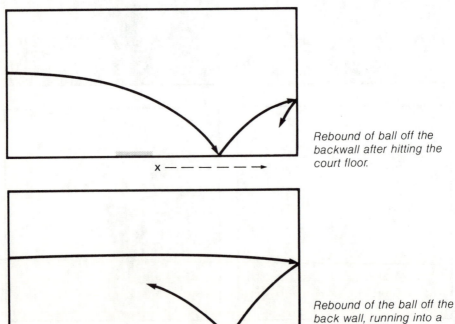

Rebound of ball off the backwall after hitting the court floor.

Rebound of the ball off the back wall, running into a center court position.

for the ball to hit the floor before making contact with it. But be prepared to move forward in the court, because the ball will rebound sharply off the wall and "run" toward the front-court area. In either case, you need to position yourself so that at the point of contact, the ball will be hit off the forward foot with the proper forehand or backhand stroking motion.

Backhand return off back wall.

A more difficult shot to return is the back-wall rebound of a lob or ceiling shot that just grazes the back wall and falls to the floor. With either shot, the ball has already touched the floor. Therefore, the ball must be hit immediately after contact with the back wall. The only way to successfully hit this type of rebound is with a sharp wrist snap on the racquet. Station the racquet between the path of the ball and the wall. As the ball passes the face of the racquet, flip

*Back wall shot off a
ball grazing back wall.*

the racquet forward with a sharp wrist motion. Aim the ball to hit a high defensive shot on the front wall so that a weaker shot will still make contact somewhere on this surface. In addition, a defensive return will give you time to reposition yourself on the court.

If during a game these shots are not successfully returned, you may have to hit the ball as it is falling toward you before it strikes the back wall. In this case, the best stroke to use is an overhead ceiling shot (see page 49). With this return, you will keep the ball in play and have an opportunity to later win the rally.

Never jump to hit these balls. All balls will eventually fall to within arm's reach. If the ball hits so high off the back wall that it can't be hit with an outstretched arm, wait for the rebound. Jumping only adds another factor to control when trying to hit the ball perfectly. Jumping for the ball is a sign of IMPATIENCE.

Points to Remember:

1. To hit a ball off the back wall, pivot 90 degrees to the side from which the shot is to be taken, and cross-step forward or backward to a court position where the ball will rebound past you.
2. Watch the ball at all times by turning your head.
3. If the ball touches the floor before the back wall, the rebound will drop close to the back wall.
4. If the ball hits the back wall before touching the floor, the ball will rebound into a mid- to center-court position.

5. Balls that rebound strongly off the back wall can be returned with a defensive or offensive shot using either a backhand or forehand stroke.
6. Hitting a ball that grazes the back wall should be returned by emphasizing the wrist snap and placing the racquet along the wall, hitting a defensive return as the ball falls past the face of the racquet.

Hitting into the Back Wall

A temptation for a beginning player who has learned to rely on the back wall is to hit the ball into this wall rather than hitting it forward off the rebound. This type of hit is more likely to occur if the player turns completely around to face the back wall when playing the rebound. For some players, hitting into the back wall becomes a favorite shot. Unfortunately, the more this shot is relied on, the weaker your game will be. First, it is impossible to hit an offensive shot off an "into-the-back-wall" hit. Second, even defensive shots are unreliable from this return because you are facing away from the front wall, making it almost impossible to "aim" the ball. Finally, with the distance the ball must travel (more than the full length of the court), the ball becomes a slow-moving, easy target for your opponent to return. Thus, hitting the ball into the back wall should only be used as a "last resort shot," when there is no other way of keeping the ball in play.

The only two occasions where this situation is likely to occur (short of your moving lazily to a good court position) is (1) off a passing shot that beats you into the back court and (2) a ball that falls so close to the back wall from a ceiling, lob, or served ball that you cannot place your racquet between it and the wall to stroke it forward.

If a back wall hit must be used, contact the ball with an upward scooping motion to angle the rebound above your head and high toward the front wall. Never hit the ball from a mid- or center-court position to the back wall; your opponent will very likely be in the path of the moving ball. Standing only 10 to 15 feet away from the ball gives your opponent very little time to duck. Many serious injuries have resulted from this type of play.

The player who wants to win at racquetball cannot afford to rely on such an ineffective and dangerous shot. To avoid placing

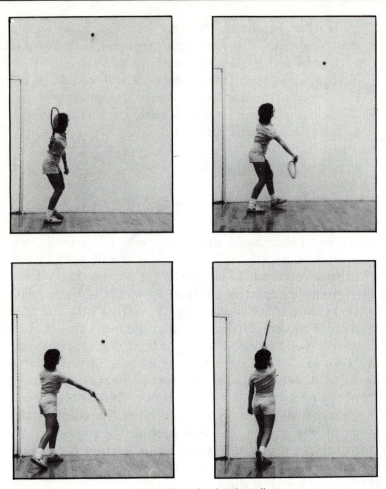

Hitting into the back wall.

yourself in the position of hitting the ball into the back wall, re-member (1) never turn 180 degrees to face the back wall to return a ball and (2) move quickly to meet the ball in the court rather than being caught out of position with no other shot available.

Points to Remember:

1. Hitting into the back wall is a desperation shot and provides little advantage to the player except to keep the ball in play.
2. Hitting into the back wall should never be done from a center- or mid-court position.
3. When returning the ball to the back wall, use a scooping stroke to lift the ball over your head and past your face.

Corner Shots

Another important return to learn is hitting a ball that rebounds to a back corner. For most players, this is the most difficult shot in the game. To contact the ball, you must contend with the back and side walls simultaneously. Without any room to stroke the ball, an effective offensive return is eliminated, and you can only hope for a down-the-line ceiling shot.

It is important with a corner shot to pivot immediately toward the corner in which the ball will rebound while keeping the ball in view. The success of this return is dependent upon your ability to position yourself properly in relation to the ball's movement. Anticipate the ball's rebound, and maintain a court position behind the forward bounce. From this position, you can still step into the ball to make contact. If the ball does not rebound with enough force

Hitting out of the corner.

to allow you to hit the ball with a forward swing, then the power in the hit must come from the wrist snap.

The key to a successful corner shot return is having the patience to wait for the ball to rebound off the back wall. Most beginners do not have the patience to wait and swing wildly as the ball comes within reach. Another mistake commonly made is using a wide, sweeping swing with an extended arm, using the shoulder to supply the force behind the stroke. Not only is this "big" arm swing dangerous, but there is no room for this type of "tennis" stroke in the corner of the court.

Contact with a corner hit that has little rebound off the back wall should be made with an open racquet face. This will direct the ball toward the ceiling and force a defensive return. If the ball rebounds away from the back wall, any forehand or backhand return can be used. Most players, however, choose a defensive return because of their back-court position. Therefore, the return of a corner ball should be considered successful if a good defensive shot is hit.

Points to Remember:

1. For all corner shots, position yourself behind the rebound so that you can step into the ball to return it.
2. Avoid using a big arm swing, especially if the ball is rebounding tightly into the corner; instead, rely on a wrist snap.
3. If the ball does not rebound strongly out of the corner, hit a defensive ceiling shot rather than trying for an offensive return.
4. A ball that rebounds hard off the corner may be returned with any type of shot.

Common Errors and How to Correct Them

1. When I try to return a ball from a back corner, my racquet always hits a side wall.

   A. You are using a large arm swing to hit the ball rather than relying on the wrist snap. Place the racquet along the anticipated path of the ball, and contact the ball when it moves past the racquet face using a sharp wrist snap.

2. When I hit a rebound off the back wall, my return always hits a side wall.

   A. Check to see if you are turning your hips to face the back wall rather than only making a pivot toward the side wall. This body position will cause you to hit the ball into a side wall rather than forward.

   B. When hitting the ball, the racquet face may also be directed at a side wall if you are contacting the ball either behind or too far in front of your forward foot. Try repositioning yourself when hitting a back-wall shot so that contact is made with the ball in proper position relative to your body.

Chapter Seven

Putting the Strokes Together: Non-Thinking Strategy

As a beginning player on the court, your strategy is limited by your skill level. As you become more proficient with a variety of shots and feel confident enough to use them in a game situation, your strategy will change accordingly. However, for the most immediate success on the court with beginning skills, a defensive strategy should be followed. This means that your objective during each rally is to keep the ball in play with defensive shots while maintaining a good court position. Points, therefore, are won with this strategy, not because you make an outstanding offensive shot, but because your opponent makes errors in his/her return. At the beginning level, unforced errors account for over half of the points scored. Therefore, if you can keep the ball in play with defensive shots, the odds are on your side that your opponent will lose the rally. This may not be as satisfying as hitting a winning shot, but it is more productive in the end. This is called the "non-thinking" strategy because few decisions are made during play. The only decision that you must make is WHICH defensive shot to hit.

Why are defensive shots a good choice for a beginning player? Simply because these shots are easiest to learn and consistently hit correctly. Defensive shots can be hit hard or soft from anywhere on the court, and there is more room for error in their placement while still being strategically effective. However, to successfully play a defensive game, several points should be remembered.

Concentrate and Watch the Ball

To follow any strategy when playing racquetball, you must concentrate on the game and watch the ball. Any mental distrac-

Concentrate and watch the ball.

tions should be left outside the court to improve your concentration on the game for the players' safety and the fun of the game. A player who is distracted by other thoughts may find him/herself at the painful end of a stroke, or at the very least playing below his/her skill level.

Part of concentrating on the game requires that you watch the ball at all times. This is true regardless of whether it is your turn to hit the ball or not. The movement of the ball is so fast around the court and has the potential to quickly change directions that losing eye contact with the ball usually results in an inability to properly "set up" for the stroke in time. Therefore, your return often results in loss of a point because of an unforced error.

Moving and watching the ball.

Serve Your Best

Even though you are following a defensive strategy, you can and should use your serve to its offensive advantage. This means: serve your best. "Best" can be defined in two ways: (1) either the serve that you hit well with predictable results or (2) the serve that may not be skillfully hit but attacks the opponent's weakness in service return. How should you choose between these two options? Usually, the choice is automatic. If a particular type of serve (i.e., lob to the backhand side) always gains a point for you through a faulty return, then use it. If your opponent has no consistent weakness with one type of serve, then use your most skillful serve — one that is always properly placed and hit with authority.

Unfortunately, when playing a new opponent, it will take time and possibly some "lost serves" before you can discover a player's weakness or which serve is working best for you that day. In this case, a good strategy is to serve to the opponent's backhand. For most beginning players, the backhand suffers from a lack of practice because forehand strokes are hit with more success. Therefore, backhand strokes are not as skillfully controlled.

Serve to the back corner.

In addition to hitting toward the backhand side, the effectiveness of any serve can be increased if the ball is hit so that the rebound lands close to a side wall in a back corner. This court position makes the serve more difficult to return with an offensive stroke. Another benefit of this serve placement is that your opponent must move from the middle of the court to return the ball. Consequently, this court position is open for you to occupy.

If you are still confused as to how to serve the ball, use your own experience as a guide. The serve that is most difficult for you to return will be the most difficult for your opponent as well, assuming that both of you are at similar skill levels. Remember — your service strategy does not suggest that a serve is only successful if it is an "ace." Rather, the serve is useful if a weak return follows (i.e., a ball that is neither an offensive nor a good defensive shot). This type of return sets you up for an easy offensive shot to the front wall and a point.

Keeping a Center Court Position

In a game involving beginning players, balls often pass through the center court after rebounding off the front wall. This is because the novice player returns most balls to the center of the front wall. Therefore, standing 1 to 3 feet behind the short line and an equal distance from either wall will give you the best position to reach most balls. A center-court position is suggested not only because more balls travel through this area than any other part of the court, but from here, the player can reach balls that rebound short or long or that run along either wall.

How do you gain and maintain this strategic center-court position? If you are serving, the problem is easily solved. When playing singles, the server usually serves from a position close to the center of the service area. This position is taken for two

Center court position.

Service position in service zone.

reasons. First, if all serves are hit from the same place in the service area, there is little chance of the server's court position "giving away" the type of serve that he/she is going to hit. Second, this position allows easy access to the strategic playing position in center court. As soon as the server is allowed to leave the service area, he/she should back up into this area. Because of the server's proximity to center court, a few quick steps will do the job. Unfortunately, beginning players often choose to turn, face the back wall (and the receiver who is hitting the ball), and move to a center-court position while "watching" the serve. Not only is this dangerous because it exposes the server to a direct "in-the-face" return off the receiver's racquet, but a quick return of serve may find the server with his/her back to the front wall as the ball rebounds. Thus, backing up to center court while using peripheral vision to follow the ball is not only the safest, but the most effective tactic.

Maintaining this court position after the serve is merely a matter of keeping your opponent out of it. To do this, consistently place your shots so that the rebound off the front wall is wide of the middle of the court and deep into a back-court position. A ceiling, lob, or high Z ball are all effective in placing the ball deep into a back-court corner. To return these shots, your opponent must follow the ball to the back court, leaving the center-court position open for you to occupy. As long as your returns are hit in this manner, the center court will always be open.

One precaution that beginners must be aware of is to avoid hitting the ball hard enough to allow it to rebound off the back wall and into the center court. Since the player hitting the ball cannot be impeded by the opponent, a rebound of this type would force you to move out of a center-court position.

Similarly, if you are receiving the serve, hitting a defensive stroke (such as the ceiling, lob, or high Z) along a side wall into a back corner or even a down-the-line return will open the center court as the server chases your return. Therefore, you should be ready to move to the center-court position once your opponent has vacated this area. The usual movement on a racquetball court consists of a constant shifting of position in and out of the center court.

Moving the server out of a center court position.

Thus the non-thinking strategy suggests returning to the center-court position after each shot as quickly as possible, or maintaining this position until moving for a ball forces you out. At the same time, continue to hit defensive shots away from the midline of court to keep your opponent out of this strategic court position.

Moving to the Ball

The reason why you can move your opponent out of center-court position is simply because he/she must leave center court to play the ball. Unfortunately, many beginning players are content to hit the ball if it is within an arm's reach regardless of where the ball is in relation to their body. This means using unorthodox strokes, few of which a player has practiced. Returns hit in this way will serve only to rebound the ball to the front wall rather than place it. This tactic keeps the ball in play but provides neither an offensive nor a defensive advantage. Since you have practiced hitting fore-hand and backhand shots, why not use them! The key to success in racquetball is not only knowing where to hit the ball to keep your opponent at a disadvantage, but being able to do it. Using tried and true strokes will produce better game results than a contrived, over-the shoulder "punch."

To hit the ball with the same stroke requires that you move to a court position where the best contact with the ball can be made. Usually, this strategy involves playing balls off the back wall to allow the ball to drop from shoulder height as it moves through the court to a lower position off the back wall rebound. Low balls can be hit with the same forehand and backhand strokes by bending your knees and dropping your waist closer to the ground. The stroking technique remains the same.

Instead of waiting for the ball to drop from an overhead position to within arm's reach, however, many beginning players jump to reach the ball. Jumping is never advised as a means of getting to a ball for three reasons. First, all balls will eventually fall to the floor and could be hit from waist level. Second, jumping for the ball prevents you from stepping into the stroke and generating more power in the swing. Third, the jumping is another factor that must be controlled to hit a good return. Therefore, jumping is neither necessary nor practical as a means of moving to the ball. This is one situation where you must wait for the ball to come to you.

Finally, when adjusting your court position to move to the ball for the best hit, it is important to move where the ball will be rather than chasing the ball around the court. Always take the shortest and most direct path to the ball's rebound. If you find this hard to do, spend some time in a court alone, hitting the ball at various angles into the front wall, and watch the ball's movement. For

Moving directly to the ball.

beginning players who have not played a court game before, the rebound angles and movement of the ball must be learned through experience.

Playing the Defensive Game

In summary, playing the defensive game does not mean that the beginning player should never hit an offensive shot. Rather, this strategy tries to simplify the game by minimizing the options available to the player. To some extent, these options are already minimized by the skill of the player and the type of shot available. If an offensive shot can be made successfully, by all means use it to end the rally. However, the beginning player usually must concentrate on merely "staying in the game" and "keeping the ball in play," especially with a more experienced opponent. The defensive game is designed to do this. In general, the defensive game relies only on your ability to hit a defensive shot and keep your opponent away from the offensive center-court position. This means consistently hitting high lobs, high Z balls, or three-wall shots to a back corner while maintaining the center-court position yourself. In this type of game you do not "win" the game so much as the opponent "loses" it. Regardless, you are still the victor. This is "non-thinking" strategy, because your return to the front wall is predetermined before the ball leaves your racquet — a defensive shot to the opponent's backhand corner.

The other part of the "non-thinking" strategy is your court position. Except for the time when you are moving to hit the ball, always station yourself in the offensive center-court position. This means that as soon as the ball leaves your racquet and you can move without interfering with your opponent, return (if necessary) to the center-court position. Too often, a beginning player hits the ball and remains stationary, waiting to see where the opponent will hit the ball. If you are positioned on one side of the court and/or in the fore or back court, you are "giving away" part of the court. A ball hit to the opposite side, short or long, would be almost impossible to return. Therefore, hit the ball and MOVE. Where? To the center court.

This strategy is not only practical for the beginner, but for any player who is facing a stronger, quicker, and perhaps more skilled opponent. The defensive game takes away the opponent's offensive opportunities and slows the tempo of the game. If you are not able to move fast enough to position yourself for good returns, then hitting a defensive return will help to slow the ball's movement and provide more time to get in position for the ball.

Women can find a defensive game especially effective against men. Usually men are stronger and faster and hit the ball with more power. Forcing the man to always return off slower-moving defensive shots will minimize this advantage. In addition, the defensive shot will give you some "breathing room" — time to reposition yourself in the center court and "catch your breath."

Points to Remember:

1. The defensive game is not designed for you to win points, but rather to prevent you from losing points.
2. Begin on the offensive with your best serve or at least with a serve that will prevent your opponent from hitting an offensive return.
3. After the serve, move to the center-court position, and return to it after each hit.
4. Hit defensive shots on all your returns and preferably to the opponent's backhand, if that is his/her weak side.
5. Realize that defensive shots can also slow down the game and help to maintain the playing tempo at a speed at which you can successfully compete.
6. Use offensive shots only if they are "sure" winners; otherwise, you are "giving" away a point.

Chapter Eight

Putting the Strokes Together: Thinking Strategy

The "non-thinking" strategy of the defensive game becomes ineffective as a player's skills improve. When a player is able to add offensive strokes to his/her game with a predictable outcome, a "thinking strategy" must be used. The strategy in this type of game not only involves keeping the opponent out of an offensive court position, but takes advantage of the opponent's weaknesses in skill or court position through ball placement and shot selection.

During this game, shots are varied but purposeful. This is a THINKING strategy that calls for the player to use a variety of defensive and offensive shots. Thus, points are won rather than lost, and the style of play is more aggressive. How successful a thinking/offensive strategy can be depends upon the skill level of the players.

How to Choose the Right Serve

Minimally, the "right" serve is one in which an offensive shot is not returned. Ideally, the "right" serve results in no return to the front wall or in such a weak return that the server can hit a winning shot immediately. Which serve will be most effective in achieving these goals will vary from opponent to opponent.

It is always a good strategy to begin by hitting your best serve to your opponent's backhand. Even if he/she is anticipating a ball to this side, the skill of your serve should still score a point. Relying continually on this serve, however, will only give your opponent an opportunity to practice returning it until he/she gets it right! Thus, variety in your serves will be the ultimate key to success at this level of play. How can you add variety to the serve? Changing the speed of the serve, the height to the front wall, the rebound angle to the back court, or the depth to which the ball is hit in the court will all

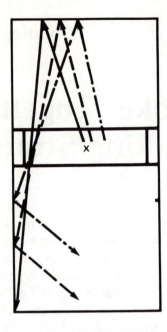

Changing the angle of the serve will cause a change in the depth of the rebound into the back court.

give your serve a "new look." The same basic serve can be hit to either side, short or long, high or low, hard or slow. In general, low, hard-hit serves (like the drive, low Z) are more effective in "forcing" a poor return; however, this type of serve is more difficult to control. High, softer serves such as the lob, high Z, and garbage serve are not as difficult to hit and, due to their placement, result in a ceiling shot return rather than an offensive shot.

Choosing the most effective serve for the game situation varies from service to service and depends on how well you are playing. If the strengths of your game outnumber the strengths of your opponent, you can play your hard serve (drive, low Z) knowing that your skill should win the point. If the opponent's strengths outnumber yours, then you need to play to his/her weaknesses and serve for a defensive return. Continue to keep your opponent on the defensive until an offensive opportunity opens for you. Consequently, the type of serve that you choose will set the tone for your game strategy: attack and try to outgun your opponent or play a more conservative game that keeps the opponent off the offensive.

You may also serve effectively to your opponent's forehand. Many players practice serving only to the backhand side. Serving only to this side of the court will take away some of the variety in your serve and allow your opponent to anticipate where the ball will be directed.

Serving to the forehand side.

A serve to the forehand side can be effective if it is properly hit and wide of center. If this is your opponent's strong stroke, then do not serve a hard-hit ball to his/her forehand. Rather, use a lob or high Z serve to force a defensive return. If your opponent does not have a strong forehand shot, a low drive serve will usually force a down-the-line return on the same side of the court. If you anticipate this return and position yourself a step closer to the side wall, your second shot of the rally can be a winner. Therefore, a serve can also be effective if the return of that serve "sets" you up for an offensive shot regardless of how well the return of serve is hit.

Another rule of strategy suggests that when you are tired, hit your hardest serves. Assuming that you are not the player in worse shape, your feeling of fatigue will undoubtedly be matched by your opponent. The harder the serve, the faster it must be reacted to. A tired player reacts slower and/or returns the ball with less power than the fresh opponent. Take advantage of your ability to control the tempo of the game by serving hard and keeping up the pressure. This would be an excellent time to hit a short drive serve if your opponent is playing deep in the back court.

Remember — with the serve, you control the game. It is the only time during play when you determine where the ball will be when you hit it. Use this advantage to set the tempo of the game, emphasize your strong skills, and force your opponent to rely on his/her weaknesses. At the very least, if a point is not won with the serve, you must be sure that it is not LOST because of a weak serve.

Short drive serve.

Anticipating Your Opponent's Shot

The beginning player is restricted to playing from a center-court position during a rally due to his/her inability to anticipate ball movement and/or lack of playing skill. Most shots can be easily hit from the center court, and most poorly placed balls generally rebound to this area. Therefore, it is an ideal location for the novice player. The experienced player, however, is usually facing an opponent whose shot selection is varied, and ball control allows more skill in court placement. Thus, rather than "playing the court," as the beginning player does, the more experienced player plays the shot. This means that you should anticipate the best return that your opponent can hit given his/her skill level, and begin moving for the ball's predicted path before it is hit.

Anticipating a shot is not always guesswork. Many players will "signal" the kind of shot that they are going to make merely by their body position relative to the ball. Since you are watching the ball at all times, you can simultaneously watch your opponent set up to hit the ball. Notice changes in stance (hip and foot placement), racquet head angle, and court position (i.e., close to a back wall or in center court). Look for any body or racquet position that is consistent with one particular shot. If nothing is apparent but you are continually beaten by one particular return, use the game situation and court position as a guide as to when that shot would be used, then move to cover it.

*Racquetball angle indicating
a ceiling or Z-ball return.*

To help anticipate the ball's movement, especially how hard the ball is hit, use your ears as well as your eyes. The sound of the ball hitting the racquet can give you a clue as to the power of the stroke. A strong hit will make a louder sound against the strings of the racquet than an easy return or mis-hit. Listen to the sound of the hit to anticipate how hard and fast the ball will rebound off the front wall.

Using the Court Wisely

A player's court position can be used to his/her advantage in two ways. One is to "take away" the opponent's "best shot" — that shot which has a high probability of being a winner — and the second is to keep your opponent moving in the court with the purpose of tiring him/her out.

The first use of the court requires that you maintain a court position to either (1) make your opponent's best return shot impossible to hit or (2) place you in the ideal position to return the ball off this return. This tactic is only important when your opponent has been successful in scoring consistently off one return. To prevent losing more points to this shot, you must in essence "block" it. An example of blocking a shot would be staying to the left of center to "discourage" a down-the-line shot in order to force a weaker cross-court return. To be effective in "blocking" shots, however, your court position must be fixed before the opponent returns the ball — otherwise no blocking has occurred. Remember — the purpose of positioning yourself on the court in this manner is to eliminate this shot as one of your opponent's options.

The object of the second use of the court is to literally keep your opponent running. Shot selection is determined not only by the other player's weaknesses, but also with consideration as to how far he/she would have to move to get to the ball. For example, if you have just hit the ball to the backhand side, return the ball to the forehand side. Varying placement of the ball short and long is also effective if your opponent has not anticipated the short ball and set up for this return. Even the most conditioned player will fatigue after long rallies where the ball must be hit from all parts of the court. This tactic can be especially valuable at the end of the game when fatigue causes slower reaction and movement times.

Blocking a down-the-line return.

"Returning" to the Offensive Position

Since the serve provides the server with the first opportunity to score, the server is considered to be the offensive player. As such, he/she is initially in control of the game. Thus, it is the job of the receiver to regain the serve and thus the offense. The first step in this strategy requires that you move the opponent out of the center-court position. Any of the defensive strokes or a down-the-line or cross-court return will work equally as well. The preference for the latter two shots is that they are offensive returns and have the potential for ending the rally immediately. However, neither of these strokes should be hit unless the ball is served at knee level or below. Balls that are served high off the front wall or that rebound high into the back court (lob, Z ball, ceiling) should be hit with your best defensive return. With any of these returns, the server will be pulled out of the center-court position, which you can now assume. Consequently, you have eliminated the server's offensive court advantage and regained this position yourself.

To make the best return possible off serves that rebound off the floor high against the back wall, make it a practice to hit the serves as soon after the floor bounce as possible. If you allow the ball to strike the back wall, you must hit the ball as it falls to the floor, possibly very close to the corner. Hitting the serve before it touches the back wall will usually give you a better shot opportunity. Similarly, balls that would "run the corner" should be taken before the corner is hit. Otherwise, you will face a very difficult return. This may mean positioning yourself a step or two closer to the front wall and away from the back wall to catch the bounce.

"Returning" to the offensive can be done in two ways: (1) either hit a winning shot off the return (kill or passing shot) or (2) hit a defensive shot that forces the server to leave the center-court position. The choice of the return will usually depend on the choice of serve. A low ball (below your knee) is a prime candidate for an offensive return; a high ball above your shoulder, a defensive shot. Those balls falling in between should either be taken before dropping below shoulder level or hit after falling below the knee. Balls that rebound off the floor to the back wall should be taken after the floor bounce.

Hitting a Winning Shot

A shot can result in a score for one of three reasons: (1) the ball was hit so well that the opponent could not return it even though he/she was in proper court position (kill shot); (2) the ball was hit to an area of the court that the opponent could not reach in time to return the ball (passing shot); and (3) the opponent just missed the ball — an unforced error. The third reason for a score may be related to your play only if you had consistently hit for long rallies with defensive shots to tire out the opposing player. Otherwise, unforced errors must be considered as being due to a mental lapse on your opponent's part, and you cannot take credit for the point.

However, the first and second reasons for a winning shot depend upon your play. To hit a winning shot, you must be aggressive. Always move quickly to the ball, and align yourself correctly for the proper hit. Never wait for the ball to come to you or be satisfied with hitting the ball if it happens to be within reach if you can maneuver for a better shot.

There are three times when you can consider hitting the ball as it rebounds from the front wall (see page 23). Which you choose depends on how aggressively you are playing and whether you want to speed up or slow down the game. The first is after the ball comes off the front wall and before it hits the floor. Hitting a volley is very effective at speeding up play and possibly catching your opponent out of court position. The best return for a winning shot off a volley is a cross-court or down-the-line passing shot. Care must be taken, however, not to hit the pass so hard that the ball rebounds off the back wall into the center-court playing area.

If you choose to let the ball bounce, it may be hit immediately after touching the floor as it passes between your shoelaces and knee or after the height of the arch is reached and the ball is falling to the floor, passing again through this same area. Aggressive players try to take most balls on the "skip," just after the floor is hit. This also works to speed up play and may catch the opponent out of court position. In addition, it offers the advantage of being at the right position from which to hit a kill shot.

Waiting until the ball arches and is falling for the second time to the floor not only gives you more time to set up for the shot, but for the opponent to set up for the return as well. Therefore, hitting the ball at this point should be primarily done by the beginning player who reacts slowly to the ball or by the experienced player who is trying to slow down the game.

Regardless of where you are when you hit the ball or what kind of ball you hit, move to cut off your opponent's anticipated return after you hit the ball. There you will be the least vulnerable to your opponent's next shot, and you can begin to set up for another winning return.

Sometimes a Good Defense is the Best Offense

Every player will meet someone who is his/her match against the best serves or who can anticipate the ball's movement in the court and can score at will. Often this occurs when women play men who are more experienced court players and who, due to the speed and power of the strokes, seem to be playing in a different time zone.

The only way to make a game of this situation is to try to outmaneuver the power. This can be done in three ways: (1) slow the ball and tempo of the game by waiting to hit the ball just before the second bounce and by hitting defensive shots; (2) use defensive return shots to the opponent's weak side and hit garbage serves; and (3) keep your opponent out of the center court by hitting balls wide of the midline. Trying to outgun power usually leads to a sloppy game, referred to as "Battleball" (see page 75). However, using a strategy that never gives your opponent anything "good" to hit or a court position from which to hit it eliminates the power as a factor.

Garbage serve to the backhand.

Thus, the best offense for some experienced players against a power player is a good defensive game. It may not have the spark and strong rallies of a power game, but the weaker player who is the tactician will have a chance to score.

This is not to imply that the player can never hit offensive shots, but rather that these shots should only be attempted when there is a high probability of success. Indeed, the defensive game should be used to tire out the opponent by moving him/her around the court, frustrate him/her into an unforced error, or solicit a weak return that sets up your offensive shot. The name of this game is patience — patience to endure the long rallies and wait for your opening to an offensive position. Above all, to use this strategy effectively, you must be careful never to hit a low ball to your opponent's strong side, since that is just the oportunity needed to begin a power game.

Winning When You Are Not the Best Player

Playing the Weakness

Every player has a weakness — a shot that he/she would prefer not to hit. Your job is to find that weakness and take advantage of it if you can. If the opponent does not appear to have a weakness, create one through ball placement and court position. A player who is constantly running to hit a ball will fatigue no matter how good he/she is, so keep the ball moving. If indeed the player is much stronger than you, then go for broke. Try to hit everything and anything, even the best kill shot. If you concede the shot, the point is lost; if you try for the ball, you may just return a few and stop a rally. If nothing else, Mr. Sharpshooter may think twice about his choice of hits, knowing that you came close to returning a ball. This hesitancy may cause some mis-hits and provide better opportunities for making offensive returns.

However, to have any hope that this strategy will succeed, give yourself the best chance for hitting a winner. Never hit the ball and hold court position. MOVE to cut off his/her return, and HUSTLE. If this strategy doesn't work, at least you put up a fight.

Points to Remember:

1. Play an offensive game, plan your shots, and move your opponent around the court to set up your best return.
2. Vary your serves by changing the force of the hit, the angle off the front wall, and where the balls rebound behind the short line.
3. Anticipate your opponent's shot, and move to a court position to block it and/or set up for the return.
4. Use defensive shots from the back-court position and offensive returns from a center- or front-court position.
5. Keep your opponent away from a center-court position by hitting balls wide of the midline of the court and into the back corners.
6. When you are tired, hit harder and move faster.
7. When playing a stronger opponent, play a defensive game and slow the tempo of play.

Chapter Nine

Drills For The Aspiring Player

Racquetball drills are useful in helping the beginning player develop the skills necessary to play the game and in giving the experienced player opportunity to practice and sharpen his/her shots. Drills may also be used as a part of your warm-up routine to help you get the "feel" for the court and the ball's movement as well as help to adjust your body to exercise.

The following list of drills was designed to provide the player with an opportunity to work on the strokes and shots used most often in a game situation. Evaluative measures are given with some drills to help you determine your proficiency with that skill and when you would be ready to incorporate it into your game plan.

The drills are listed from the most basic skills to playing modified games with an opponent. The beginning player can either start with the first drill and work through to the simulated games or pick the drills that work on the skills with which he/she is having the most difficulty.

In all drills, starting the ball in play is critical. The ball can be either dropped or tossed against a wall. When dropped, you must be sure to drop the ball in front of your forward foot so that you can step into the stroke when contacting the ball. If the ball is tossed to a wall, position yourself so that the rebound falls in front of your body position. This will allow you to step forward to meet the ball. The wrong ball toss will result in learning to stroke at a ball that is improperly positioned in relation to your body.

Scoring scales are presented in selected drills. The illustrations accompanying these drills indicate the size of the target area (1' or 2') and the score allotted to each target zone (5, 3, or 1 points). Balls in the targeted area can be scored by "guess," or small pieces of masking tape can be placed on the floor and walls to outline the areas. Balls that hit a line between 2 point areas should be given the lower of the 2 scores. A legal return not hitting the target area is scored 0 points. Although the target points are somewhat arbitrary, they do identify, through points scored, the accuracy and placement of your shots. In general, the following scoring percentages can be used to determine the effectiveness of your returns and serves:

90 to 100 percent of the total points: "bread and butter shot; use this shot whenever your strategy dictates.

75 to 89 percent of the total points: consistent enough to use to vary your shots; a dependable shot in a game where you are in control.

50 to 74 percent of the total points: be careful — you may miss this shot half of the time; not the shot to choose when the game is close but a good shot to practice when you can afford to lose some points.

below 50 percent of the total points: POISON — do not hit this in a game situation because you will miss it more than half of the time.

Drill I: Watching the Game

Purpose: To develop a concept of how racquetball is played and the use of offensive and defensive shots during the game.

Method: Go to a court with an observation area, and watch experienced players play racquetball. Count the number of offensive and defensive shots used by each player.

Drill II: Forehand Shots

Purpose: To practice hitting a forehand shot to the back corners of the court from three primary areas of the floor.

Method: Hit 8 balls each from the mid-, center-, and back-court positions. From each position, hit 4 balls to the back right corner and 4 balls to the back left corner. Hit the ball after you have dropped it to the floor.

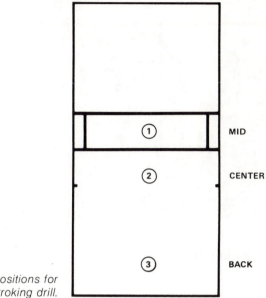

Hitting positions for stroking drill.

Drill III: Backhand Shots

Purpose: To practice hitting a backhand shot to the back corners of the court from 3 primary areas of the floor.

Method: Hit 8 balls each from the mid-, center-, and back-court positions. From each position, hit 4 balls to the back right corner and 4 balls to the back left corner. Hit the ball after you have dropped it to the floor.

Drill IV: Forehand and Backhand Shots from Side-wall Toss

Purpose: To practice hitting forehand and backhand shots to the back corners of the court from a ball bouncing off the side wall.

Method: Stand with your hips pivoted and facing the side wall appropriate for either a forehand or backhand stroke. Toss the ball into the side-wall. After the rebound, hit the ball to a back corner of the court. Hit 8 balls from each of the 3 court positions, then repeat 8 shots each from the same court positions with the other stroke.

Toss off of the side wall.

Drill V: Suicide Drill

Purpose: To develop muscular endurance and anaerobic capacity, and to practice moving to the ball and returning it to the front wall.

Method: Begin in the center court, and after dropping the ball, hit it to the front wall. Continue to return the ball as quickly as you can, hitting all balls regardless of their court position or the number of times the ball has bounced off the floor. Work at positioning yourself correctly for each hit. Continue this drill for 2-minute intervals, allowing yourself to rest 30 seconds to 1 minute after each hitting session. Continue the drill for 20 minutes.

Drill VI: 30-Second Drill

Purpose: To teach the player to react quickly to the ball's court position and improve his/her movement time, and to work on ball control.

Method: Begin in a center-court position. Drop the ball and return it to the front wall. Continue to return the ball off the rebound, counting the number of times the ball is returned in 30 seconds. Do this drill once every other practice session. Try to improve 1 to 3 shots each time.

Drill VII: Serving Drill — Lob and High Z

Purpose: To practice hitting lob and high Z serves correctly and accurately to a back-corner court position.

Method: Standing close to the center of the service zone, hit 10 lob serves to the right back corner of the court to the designated target area. Score each serve and total the points. Refer to the scoring scale to determine the accuracy of the serve. Total points

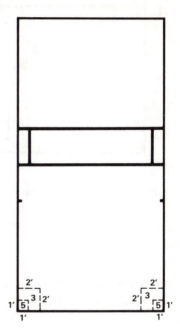

Scoring area for the lob and high Z serving drill.

possible = 50. Repeat this drill with the lob serve to the left back corner and the target area. Score and evaluate. Total points possible = 50. (Note: for a lob hit with a backhand stroke, you may move in the service area toward the backhand side wall). Repeat both parts of this drill using a high Z serve. Total points possible for each part = 50 points.

Drill VIII: Serving Drills — Drive Serve

Purpose: To develop accuracy in your drive serve and be able to drive serve to a variety of court positions.

Method: From the center of the service zone, hit 3 drive serves to each of the 4 designated court positions. Repeat the circuit three

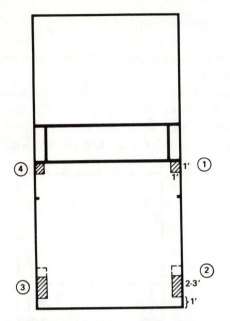

Scoring area for the drive serve.

times. Score 1 point for each correct placement. Total points possible = 36. (Note: you can total points scored to each designated area to indicate your most accurate placement. Total points to each area = 9.)

Drill IX: Defensive Shots — Lob, Ceiling, High Z, Around-the-Wall

Purpose: To practice hitting a defensive shot from 2 court positions and develop accuracy in ball placement.

Method: Using a dropped ball, hit each defensive shot 10 times from center- and back-court positions (5 to each corner). Use the same target area as designated for the lob and high Z serves. Total points possible for each serve from each position = 50. To vary this drill, begin the defensive shot with a side-wall toss.

Drill X: Back Wall Drill

Purpose: To practice hitting balls rebounding off the back wall and accurately return them wide of the midline in a back-court area.

Method: Standing in the back court, toss balls into the back wall to rebound for a forehand stroke. Hit 10 balls, returning each to the front. Score the rebound in the designated target area. Total points possible = 50. Repeat the drill using a ball toss to your backhand side, and return the balls with a backhand stroke. Total points possible = 50.

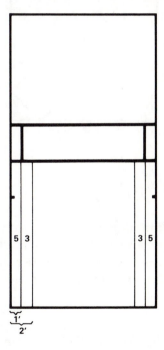

Scoring area for the back wall drill.

Drill XI: Corner Return

Purpose: To practice hitting balls after they have rebounded from a back corner and accurately return them into a back-court position wide of the court midline.

Method: Standing in the back court, toss a ball to your forehand side to rebound either from the back wall to a side wall or in the opposite direction. Return 10 balls with your forehand stroke, then turn and toss 10 balls to the opposite side/back wall for

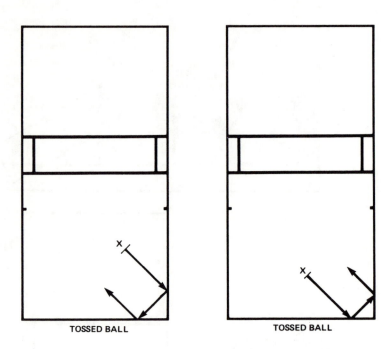

Path of a tossed ball for the corner hit drill - side wall toss.

Path of tossed ball for the corner hit drill - back wall toss.

a backhand return. Hit each ball to rebound into a back-court position and wide of the midline of the court. Score each return with the same designated target area used for the back-wall returns. Total points possible for each stroke = 50.

Drill XII: Repeat Ceiling Shots

Purpose: To practice hitting a ceiling return from any court position.

Method: Standing in a center-court position, use a side-wall toss to put the ball in play and hit 10 consecutive ceiling returns without the ball hitting the floor more than once between shots. Use the designated target area shown in the lob and high Z service drill. Total points possible = 50.

Drill XIII: Offensive Shots — Passing

Purpose: To practice hitting passing shots from 2 court positions and accurately direct them to 1 of two court areas.

Method: Using a side-wall toss to your forehand side, hit 10 passing shots from court positions, A and B. Return the ball into the

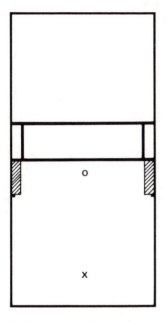 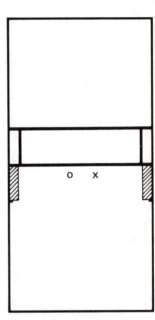

A. *Target area for a passing shot for a back court position.*

B. *Target area for a passing shot from a center court position.*

shaded area of the court diagram. Score 1 point for each successful return. Total points possible = 10. Repeat the drill using a backhand stroke. Total points possible = 10.

Drill XIV: Offensive Shots — Kill

Purpose: To practice hitting accurate kill shots from 3 court positions.

Method: Dropping the ball to your forehand side, hit 10 kill shots from each court position: A, B, and C. Score each position

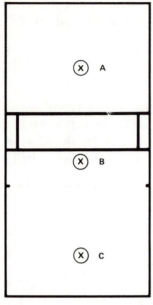

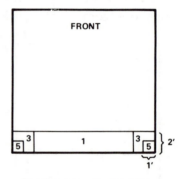

Hitting positions for the kill shot drill.

Scoring area for the kill shot drill.

separately using a front-wall target area. Use corner and pinch kill shots. Total points possible = 50. Repeat the drill using a drop to your backhand side. Total points possible = 50. This drill can also be varied by using a side-wall toss to put the ball into play.

Drill XV: Rally Drill — Hit and Move

Purpose: To practice hitting a ball and moving away from the rebound to avoid colliding with your opponent on the court.

Method: Standing side by side in the back court with your opponent, the player on the right side of the court hits a ball straight into the front wall. After hitting, this player moves to the left and out of the way of the opponent moving toward the ball. The ball is again returned straight into the front wall, and the positions are again reversed. Continue this rotation until the ball is missed.

Drill XVI: Mini Game

Purpose: To give players a chance to practice serving and re-turning the serve.

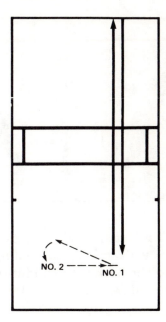

*Rally drill to avoid
collisions on the court.*

Method: Each player serves 5 times and then rotates to the back court to be the receiver. The game is to 15 points, and a point is scored by either player on each rally regardless of whether he/she was serving.

Drill XVII: Defensive Return Game

Purpose: To practice hitting a defensive shot off any serve.
Method: Only the server scores. The server must use a drive serve and the receiver a ceiling or other defensive return. If the receiver does not use this type of return, the server scores a point. If the drive serve is not hit, a side out occurs. Variation: change the type of serve required to be hit, or specify exactly which defensive shot needs to be returned.

Drill XVIII: Game Warm-Up Drill

Purpose: To provide a method for warming up before a game.
Method: Begin by standing side by side with your opponent just behind the short line. Practice hitting forehand strokes to the

Players warming up before a game.

front wall. After several minutes, move two-thirds of the way back to the back wall and practice ceiling shots from this position. Finally, back up to the back wall and hit offensive and defensive returns to the front wall from a ball toss off the back wall.

Chapter Ten

Court Etiquette
and Interpreting the Rules

As in all sport activities, there is a degree of courtesy involved in a competitive racquetball game, and there is a great need to understand and interpret the rules of the game in a fair and objective manner. With two individuals enclosed in a room of 20′ x 20′ x 40′, there is little room for disagreement. The possibility of injury and negative feelings increases if every courtesy is not extended to the opponent and if the rules are not complied with in detail.

Prior to the Start

Prior to the start of the match, the court must be shared by players executing the shots to be used in the match. In that warm-up each player needs to control ball placement to avoid interference with his/her opponent. The court should be divided in length, and all shots should be hit within that boundary. During the warm-up, players should only hit shots that they can control, and they should be considerate of the opponent if he/she must retrieve a ball hit into the front court. Stopping execution of a shot if the opponent walks in front of you or moves to your court to retrieve a ball are specific examples. Bouncing the ball back to the opponent is also appreciated and in good taste.

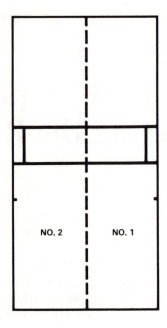

Court divided in length for warm-up.

Two players warming up side by side.

Stopping execution of a warm-up shot when a player walks in front of another player.

Bouncing the ball back to an opponent when warming up.

A second consideration prior to the match requires a selection of appropriate clothing. Appropriate wearing apparel is not only a part of safety, but also a part of etiquette and rules. The rules require a light color for all clothing, including socks, shirt, and shorts. In friendly games, players sometimes wear dark or blue clothing for something different, but in doing so, you are breaking a rule of etiquette by not giving the opposing side a fair view of the ball.

Contrast of clothing and racquetball ball.

Scoring, Serving, and Ball in Play

Use of proper etiquette and interpretation of the rules during the game is crucial to acceptable play. Some of the rules are quite simple, yet the beginning player sometimes does not initially respond to the obvious and needs to be informed of a rule that most experienced players take for granted.

How to keep score is one of those rules that is taken for granted, yet should be explained. A game is won when the first player reaches 21 points; thus, a score of 21-20 is a legal game. To win a match in most situations requires you to win the best of 3 games. If each player has won 1 game, the third game is played to 11 points, again with the need to win only by 1 point (i.e., 11-10 is a legal score). Some racquetball matches are played to 15 or 11 points in a best-of-five series, and in a class situation, a student may discover that games are played to an assortment of final points to accommodate class procedures.

There are specific *rules governing the service* in racquetball. First, the server must stand between the short line and service line — an area commonly called the service zone. The back foot of the server is permitted to touch but never rest over the short line, and neither foot is allowed to touch or go over the service line. To initiate a

*Legal position of the server
in relation to the serving zone.*

serve, the player must drop the ball and then strike it with the racquet after the ball rebounds off the floor. Following racquet contact on the serve, the ball must strike the front wall first on the fly and then carry beyond the short line. The ball must strike the floor beyond the short line before hitting the back wall, ceiling, or more than one side wall. A serve that strikes the front wall on the fly and doesn't carry beyond the short line, that hits two or more side walls, that hits the back wall on the fly, or that hits the ceiling on the fly is described as a *fault*. Common terms for a fault include a *short* for a serve that doesn't carry past the short line, a *long* for a ball that hits the back wall on the fly, and *two walls* for a serve that hits more than one side wall. A second opportunity is provided for a fault serve. A *side out* serve requires the loss of serve. Loss of serve occurs when the ball does not hit the front wall on the fly after the server hits the ball, or when two faults are served in succession. Calling the score prior to every serve is always expected in a racquetball match. The server's score is always called first, alerting your opponent that the score is agreed to by both parties unless he/she stops play to question it. Also, calling the scoring implies that the next serve is going to follow shortly, and the opponent should be ready to receive.

Once the *ball is in play,* it must be hit by each player (in singles) alternately. The ultimate goal of either player is to hit the ball so that it strikes the front wall before hitting the floor. A ball can hit the back wall, followed by the ceiling and the side walls, as long as it eventually gets to the front wall before touching the floor.

A server continues the serve for each point played until two faults are hit in succession, a side out serve is made, or the server

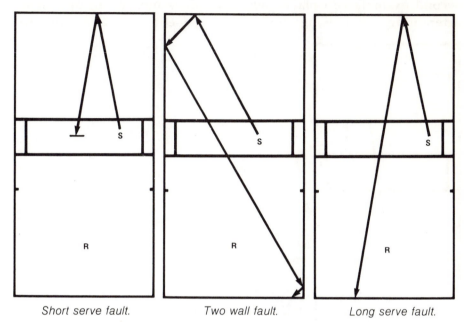

| *Short serve fault.* | *Two wall fault.* | *Long serve fault.* |

cannot return the opponent's shot in a legal manner (i.e., not returning the ball to the front wall before it strikes the floor, hitting after the second bounce, or committing an avoidable hinder). A return-of-serve player remains in that situation until the serving opponent has made one of the above-mentioned errors.

Hinders

Hinders need to be discussed in detail when interpreting the rules. There are two basic types of hinders in racquetball. The *avoidable hinders* are intentional acts of preventing an opponent from a fair try at hitting the ball. *Unavoidable hinders*, commonly called hinders, occur by accident of court play but also prevent the opponent from having a fair chance at the ball.

Avoidable hinders are usually called on a player who intentionally moves in the path of an opponent to prevent him/her from hitting the ball or seeing it clearly. Experienced players are quite skilled at avoidable hinders called *blocking*. The player committing the infraction may hit a shot from an "up" position and then set up to block the movement of the opponent in a "back" position. The movement is subtle and discourages the opponent from making an attempt to reach the ball, since he/she is "back." There are countless avoidable hinders in racquetball. The player who simply will not move to permit an opponent access to the ball is one example. A second example is a player who will move next to an opponent attempting a full-swing shot. That opponent will not be able to

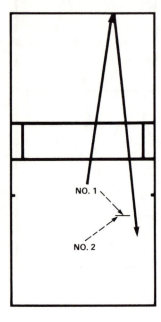

Blocking of an opponent
in the back court.

A player moving too close to a player attempting a shot.

A player who doesn't move out of the way.

A player pushing an opponent to get a ball.

complete the swing because of the position of the other player. A third example is a player pushing or shoving an opponent as a means of giving him/herself impetus to move to reach a ball. Pushing off of an opponent gives him/her an unfair advantage, since it may place the opponent in an off-balance position for the next shot. A fourth distinct violation associated with avoidable hinders is the intentional moving of the body into the path of the return shot of an opponent. If an opponent strikes the ball from a "back" position and the "up" player (recognizing that the shot would put that player at a great disadvantage for a return) moves into the path of the ball, the call is an avoidable hinder.

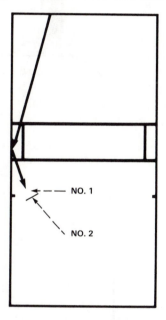

Moving into the path of an opponent, creating a hinder.

Unintentional or unavoidable hinders occur as part of the action of the game and happen without a planned effort. The first example is a *court hinder*. A court hinder occurs when the ball strikes an irregular portion of the court, such as an edge of the door, a can placed in the corner of the court, or any other part of the court that would impede the progress of play. Other examples of unintentional hinders include: (1) a player who is hit by an opponent's shot prior to the ball striking the front wall; (2) a ball that is "shadowed" so that the opponent cannot see the ball clearly; and (3) a ball that goes between the legs of the opponent, thus distracting the player hitting the ball. In addition, when two players collide attempting to move out of the way of each other or the ball, or attempting to reach the ball, play is stopped and a hinder is called.

The etiquette of calling an unavoidable hinder rests initially with the player who creates the problem. That player's obligation is to state, "Do you want a hinder?" The response from the other player is either "Yes" or "No." If a hinder is identified by the offending player, the player restricted may say "Hinder please," and

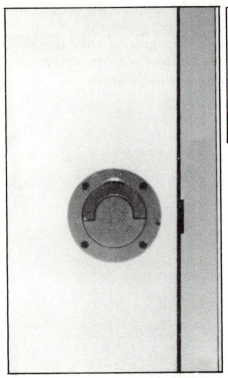

Edge of door court hinder.

A court hinder with the ball hitting a ball can.

Shadowing the ball hinder.

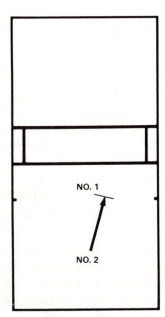

Being hit by an opponent's shot.

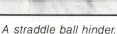

A straddle ball hinder.   *Two players colliding.*

the opposing player has only the choice of "Okay." In short, any request for a hinder is to be honored in an immediate affirmative manner. Hinders are to be requested immediately following the infraction so that no question arises concerning whether or not a hinder should be called.

An avoidable hinder results in a point loss to the opponent if the opponent was receiving and committed the infraction, and a side out if the infraction was made by the server. An unavoidable hinder requires a replay of the point. In a "friendly" game, avoidable hinders should hever happen, since the idea of the game is to play for enjoyment and fitness. If a player does resort to avoidable hinders in such an environment, a judicial response is to not play that person again.

Miscellaneous Rules

The necessary rules interpretations include the use of the racquet. Often, beginners are not aware that the racquet must be held in one hand and remain in that hand throughout any specific rally. The racquet must also be attached to the wrist by the thong in order to reduce the possibility of injury. Another interpretation that is common knowledge, but that often is misunderstood, is that the ball must always be struck only by the racquet for a legal return. Other commonly misunderstood rules include the following:

1. The ball must be dry before being placed in play.
2. A server may not take a running stride to execute the serve.
3. A receiver of serve may not cross the imaginary line until the served ball has crossed the short line, thus eliminating a potentially hazardous situation. The *imaginary five-foot line* is a three-inch vertical line placed on each side wall directly behind the short-line position.
4. A *crotch shot* strikes the floor and a wall simultaneously. During a serve, a crotch shot off the front wall is a side out serve. A crotch shot served that strikes off the back wall is in play. During play, a crotch shot is always in play unless it hits the front wall.
5. Only the server is permitted to score after a winning rally.

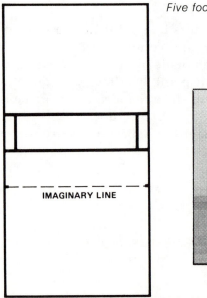

IMAGINARY LINE

Five foot imaginary line.

Vertical line describing the five foot line.

Understanding the common rules of serving, hinders, and scoring allows the novice freedom to play the game early in his/her skill development.

Doubles and Cutthroat

The singles match in racquetball is the only game recommended for safe, enjoyable play, but there are two other games associated with racquetball and rules interpretation. One is called *doubles* and should be played on a regulation doubles court that is larger than a traditional singles court. The other game, played with three players, is called *cutthroat*. Rules that relate to doubles are distinct in some ways, including serving order, player hitting order, position during serve, and hinder situations. The serve order follows a sequence of one partner serving consecutive points until a side out occurs, and then the second partner serving in a similar fashion until a second side out takes place. There is one exception to the service order of the partners, and that fits only the first serving team. The first partner serves to the conclusion of serve, then the team exchanges with the receiving team. When the first serving team returns for the second round of serves, the first serving partner again begins serve, followed by the normal sequence of partner serve rotation. The player-hitting order, once the ball is placed in play by a serve, is the same as in the singles game, with team A hitting a serve, team B returning serve, team A responding to return of serve, etc. Either player on a team may hit for that team in the rally.

During a serve, the serving team stands within the service zone as in the singles play experience. One partner serves, and the other partner is directed to stand in the service box. If the partner in the doubles box is struck by his/her partner's serve, the serve is

Doubles serve position.

declared "dead," and the serve is executed again. Once the partner steps out of the box, any ball hit by the serving partner that touches the other partner is a side out. Once the ball is in play, any ball that strikes a partner is deemed a side out or a loss of point, depending on whether the serving or receiving team committed the infraction. The receiving team must stand behind the imaginary five-foot line to receive serve. Hinders are the same as in singles play, but the possibility for hinder calls is magnified by the presence of four players on the court at one time.

The cutthroat game is an unofficial racquetball game with a safety feature built in. One cutthroat game is a two-against-one setup, with the receiving team playing as a doubles team, and the serving player competing against that team. Following each side out, the doubles team membership changes, and the server becomes a part of a new doubles team. All play on the part of the doubles team as related to movement and position utilizes doubles rules, and all other play commences as in singles. The serving rotation follows a sequence of the server as the number-one player exchanging with the number-two player, who is a receiver. When the next side out occurs, the number-two player, who has been the server, exchanges with the number-three player, who is the second receiver. The sequence follows an exchange with the number-three player (who is the server) on the next side out with the number-one player, who has moved through the sequence as receiver. Then the process is repeated. It should be noted that this type of exchange alternates the position of the receiver each time through the full serving sequence. If the number-two receiver started from a right-side receiving position during the first sequence, that number-two player would receive from the left side during the second sequence of return of serve.

The second type of cutthroat game is a safter version and becomes a singles match with three players. One player is always sitting out a particular point by standing in a back-wall area, while the other two players are playing. At the conclusion of each point, the non-competing player enters the game as a receiver of the serve, and the player who lost the point steps out. If the server loses the point, the former receiver becomes the server. If the receiver loses the point, the server remains as server, and play continues. In both games of cutthroat, each player keeps an individual score, and the winner is the first player to gain 21 points. The game of cutthroat provides for a change-of-pace situation that permits three people to enjoy a game designed for two or four.

Sportsmanship Ethic

Racquetball has a *"sportsmanship ethic"* that implies that the game is played for exercise and enjoyment. Coupled with that implication is the view that most matches are played without officiating, and it is imperative to call each point or shot fairly and without prejudice.

It is doubly important to recognize that no point is worth winning if you or your opponent are injured. The sportsmanship attitude extends to shaking hands following a match and being a "good loser" or "humble winner." The concept of sportsmanship is so much rhetoric in other sports, but in racquetball, sportsmanship is required.

Glossary of Terms in Racquetball

Ace: A legal serve that is totally missed by the receiver of the serve.

Avoidable Hinder: An intentional interference with the opponent's opportunity to play a shot fairly.

Back Court: That section of the court nearest the back wall and described as the last third of the court.

Backhand: A stroke hit from the non-racquet side of the body.

Backswing: The preparation phase of the basic swing.

Ceiling Shot: A ball that strikes ceiling-front wall or front wall-ceiling in sequence.

Center Court: The area immediately behind the short-line and equal distance from the side walls.

Closed Face: Position of the racquet face on the ball when hitting the ball downward.

Continental Grip: The grip positioned halfway between the eastern forehand and backhand grip.

Corner Kill Shot: The kill shot that strikes the front wall-side wall and rebounds in the direction of the mid court.

Cross-Court Passing Shot: A two-wall passing shot executed when the opponent is either on the same side as you or is in an "up" position. The ball hits front wall and then side wall.

Crotch: A ball that strikes 2 playing surfaces simultaneously.

Cutthroat: A 3-player racquetball game designed with the server playing against the other 2 players.

Defensive shots: Shots that prevent the opponent from holding an offensive court position.

Doubles: A 4-player racquetball game played between teams of 2 players.

Down-the-line Passing Shot: A shot that carries along a side wall 1 to 2′ from the wall and below the opponent's waist. This is also called down-the-wall, and it is designed to pass an opponent who is in an "up" position.

Eastern Forehand Grip: The conventional racquetball grip that is best described as a "shake hands" position.

Eastern Backhand Grip: The conventional backhand grip that is assumed by rotating the racquet a quarter turn to the racquet side of the body.

Fault: A serve that touches the floor before passing the short line or one in which the ball strikes the front wall and either the ceiling, the back wall, or 2 side walls before hitting the floor. These serves are illegal and must be replayed. Two faults result in a side out.

Forehand: A stroke hit from the racquet side of the body.

Front Court: That section of the court in front of the service court line.

Front Wall Kill: The kill shot that hits the front wall straight on and rebounds toward the back wall without touching a side wall.

Garbage Serve: A serve hit in between the speed of a drive and lob serve that bounces between shoulder and waist to the receiver. The serve gives an illusion of a miss-hit serve.

Goggles: Safety glasses required for wear when entering a racquetball court.

High Z Serve: A serve that strikes high off the front wall (near the ceiling) and follows a "Z" pattern across the court.

Hinder: Any situation that prevents an opponent from having a fair shot at hitting the ball during a rally. Hinders include avoidable, unavoidable, and court hinders.

Kill Shot: Any ball that strikes the front wall hard and low so that the rebound with the floor occurs almost simultaneously with the wall. A winning offensive shot.

Lob: A defensive shot, hit along a side wall so that it follows a path high over center court and falls with little rebound into a back corner. This ball may touch a side wall close to the back corner.

Long: A serve that strikes the back wall on the fly. A fault.

Match: The culmination of a competition with the winner usually winning 2 of 3 games.

Mid Court: The area between the service and short line and the two side walls.

Non-Thinking Strategy: Following a defensive reactive strategy with few decisions to make.

Offensive Shot: The attempt to win a point outright by virtue of the skill with which the shot is hit.

"On Edge": The position of the racquet face perpendicular to the floor.

Open Face: Position of the racquet face on the ball when hitting the ball up.

Overhead: Shots hit from above the shoulder position with an extended arm.

Overhead Kill: A kill shot hit from above the shoulder position.

Over-the-Shoulder: A ball hit from a position directly over the shoulder.

Passing Shot: An offensive shot that literally goes past an opponent who is in the front-, mid-, or center-court positions.

Pendulum Swing: A scooping swing used to hit balls high off the front wall or to the ceiling.

Pinch Kill: A shot that strikes the side wall-front wall sequence and that is unreturnable due to the low, high velocity of the shot. Also called a pinch shot.

Racquet Face: The portion of the racquet with which the ball is struck during play.

Rally: A continuous exchange of shots during the play of a point.

Receiving Line: The line identified by the vertical, side wall marks located 5 feet behind the short line.

"Run the Corner": A ball that rebounds to a back corner, hitting the side wall and back wall before striking floor.

Safety Hinder: A hinder called to prevent an injury.

Screen: A blocking of the opponent's vision, preventing the opponent from seeing the ball.

Service Line: The line on the floor closest to the front wall. The front line of the service zone.

Service Zone: The area between the service line and the short line. The position for the server to legally execute the serve.

Set: The ready position. The position that enables the receiver of a shot to turn or pivot to hit the ball.

Set Up: A ball that is hit so that the opponent can easily return it.

Short: A ball that does not clear the short line on the fly. A fault.

Short Line: The line on the floor nearest the back wall. The back line of the service zone.

Side Out: A loss of a serve to the opponent.

Thong: The safety strap that is attached to the racquet grip and worn around the wrist.

Thinking Strategy: The act of taking advantage of an opponent through the use of intellect, court strategy, and skill.

Three-Wall Shot: A defensive shot that rebounds off 3 walls.

Unavoidable Hinder: An unintentional interference with the opponent's opportunity to play a shot fairly.

Volley: Striking the ball in midair from a rebound off the front wall.

Wallpaper Shot: A shot that lies against the side wall, making a return extremely difficult.

Western Grip: The grip that is assumed for a forehand grip when the racquet is picked up off the floor.

Index